Acting Up in Church AGAIN

More humorous sketches for worship services

M. K. Boyle

MERIWETHER PUBLISHING LTD.
Colorado Springs, Colorado

Meriwether Publishing Ltd., Publisher
PO Box 7710
Colorado Springs, CO 80933-7710

www.meriwether.com

Editor: Rhonda Wray
Cover design: Jan Melvin

Library of Congress Cataloging-in-Publication Data

Boyle, M. K., 1961-
    Acting up in church again : more humorous sketches for worship services / by M.K. Boyle. -- 1st ed.
        p. cm.
    ISBN 978-1-56608-178-8
    1. Drama in public worship. 2. Christian drama, American. 3. Comedy sketches. I. Title.
    BV289.B68 2011
    264--dc23

                                                            2011017410

    1   2   3   11   12   13

*To my husband Jim, for cooking and caring for the children
while I sat half-comatose in front of my computer.*

*Also to my mom, Barbara Baker, who is now with the Lord.
I love you, Mom. Keep partying till I get there!*

*And to Michelle Bauer, who kept her humor while fighting cancer
and showed us what courage and love is all about.*

Contents

(In alphabetical order)

Preface

"Hey friend, how many _____s (insert your denomination here) does it take to change a light bulb?"

Hmmmm, you think. *I wonder if it's the old "one to hold the bulb and one hundred thousand to turn the house" answer. Or maybe it's "one to hold the bulb and seven to turn the ladder."*

Whether you realize it or not, I've drawn you into the story. You're snagged on my hook. You can't leave now. You're going to have to continue to read until I give you the punchline. Why is that? Quite frankly, it's because we all love a good joke — especially when we recognize that it contains a teensy bit of truth.

Here is an example. We all know that atheists do not believe in heaven or hell, so the joke goes like this: Three men enter hell. One is a Baptist, one a Catholic, and one an atheist. Satan goes over to the first man and says, "Why are you here?"

The Baptist sadly shakes his head and says, "I blew it, I'm here, that's it."

Satan goes to the Catholic and says, "What about you, boy? What do you think of your life now?"

The Catholic shrugs and says, "I'm not too worried about it because I've got someone praying me out of here."

Satan then asks the atheist, "What about you?"

The atheist says, "Man, I ain't here."

So many of us are like the atheist — denying what is real, even when that reality is staring us in the face.

One of my favorite pictures depicts Jesus surrounded by little children. One of them must have cracked a joke, because his head is turned up and he's laughing! Yes, his life's work was serious, but I'll bet even Jesus couldn't resist a chuckle or even an all-out belly laugh over a funny situation. His own ministry was characterized by frequent storytelling. First we remember the stories, and then we remember the meaning behind them.

I write because I love stories. I write mostly humorous-based pieces because I know they will be remembered longer. I love it when people approach me and say, "Remember that sketch you wrote when the pastor talked about hope?" (Or any other sermon topic.) By remembering the funny story, they remembered the message. It doesn't get much better than that!

As you explore the following pages, remember that there are no boundaries to the characters, even if their names are Suzie or Joe. A few are gender-specific (for the sake of the joke), but most of the time you may replace the names in the book with the names of your own church's actors. Enjoy, have fun, and keep laughing!

So how many _____s (your denomination) does it take to change a light bulb?

The answer is: *Change?!*

Are We There Yet?

Theme
Children, promise of God

Scripture Reference
Proverbs 22:6

Synopsis
This sketch offers words of wisdom to ward off insanity while taking children on a nature hike.

Cast
Leader
Julie
Max
As many children as desired.

Costumes
Hiking clothes

Props
Canteens, walking sticks, etc. Ask the kids to bring their school backpacks to church.

Setting
The great outdoors

Note: This was a favorite among the five- to eight-year-old children in our congregation. We heard choruses of "Are we there yet?" for weeks afterward.

1   *(JULIE and MAX are Onstage. The group LEADER enters with*
2   *KIDS behind him, lined up single file. They walk in circles around*
3   *the stage. KIDS can speak in unison or in a ripple effect. Either*
4   *way will work.)*
5   **KIDS: Are we there yet?**
6   **LEADER: No.**
7   **KIDS: Are we there yet?**
8   **LEADER: No.**
9   **KIDS: Are we there yet?**
10   **LEADER: No.**
11   **KIDS: Are we there yet?**
12   **LEADER: No.**
13   **KIDS: Are we there yet?**
14   **LEADER: No.**
15   **KIDS: Are we there yet?**
16   **LEADER:** *(Stops.)* **Yes.**
17   **KIDS: Really?**
18   **LEADER: No.**
19   **JULIE: Oh, how cute. Look at the little campers.**
20   **MAX: You must have your hands full.**
21   **LEADER: You can say that again.**
22   **JULIE: How in the world do you manage such a group?**
23   **LEADER: It's just a matter of organizational skills, being able**
24   **to ward off any potential dangers.** *(To CHILD, who has been*
25   *fidgeting with another)* **Bobby, quit pulling off Andrew's**
26   **pack.**
27   **MAX: It's a great responsibility. I don't think I could ever do it.**
28   **JULIE: Me neither.**
29   **LEADER: It's a matter of patience and remembering those wise**
30   **words from the greatest king who ever lived.**
31   **CHILD 1: Luke Skywalker?**
32   **LEADER: King Solomon.** *(Turns to one of the CHILDREN, who is*
33   *messing around with her canteen.)* **Madison, take the canteen**
34   **out of your nose.**
35   **MAX: So what does this "wise king" say?**
36   **LEADER: It's a promise, actually. He says, "Train up a child in**

1   the way he should go, and when he is old, he will not turn
2   from it" *(Proverbs 22:6).*
3   JULIE: You really believe that?
4   LEADER: I have to.
5   JULIE: Why?
6   CHILD 2: Taylor just gave Jackson a wedgie!
7   LEADER: Otherwise I would kill myself. Let's go, kids!
8   *(LEADER and KIDS start walking around the stage again.*
9   *JULIE and MAX exit.)*
10   KIDS: Are we there yet?
11   LEADER: No.
12   KIDS: Are we there yet?
13   LEADER: No.
14   KIDS: Are we there yet?
15   LEADER: No.
16   KIDS: Are we there yet?
17   LEADER: We're here! Isn't this the most fantastic waterfall
18   you've ever seen?
19   KIDS: *(Ad-lib)* Wow, cool, awesome.
20   LEADER: OK, let's head back to camp.
21   CHILD 3: But we just got here. *(All KIDS moan as they follow*
22   *group LEADER.)*
23   KIDS: Are we there yet?
24   LEADER: No.
25   KIDS: Are we there yet?
26   LEADER: No.
27   KIDS: Are we there yet? *(Repeat until all are Off-stage.)*

Art in Heaven

Theme
Heaven

Scripture Reference
John 14:2; Revelation 12:7-8, 21:19, 21

Synopsis
Two people argue about what heaven is like until
a little boy sets them straight.

Cast
Artist
Hugh
Billy

Costumes
The Artist may wear a paint shirt or smock if he or she wishes.

Props
An easel or whiteboard and paints, chalk, markers,
or whatever will work to create the picture.

Setting
Anywhere

Note: Anyone can play the Artist. The quality of the picture
doesn't matter in this performance.

1   *(The ARTIST enters and begins to draw a picture as outlined in*
2   *the script, starting with clouds. HUGH enters a few moments*
3   *later, as does BILLY from the opposite side.)*
4   **HUGH: What are you drawing?**
5   **ARTIST: Oh, hello there. I'm drawing a picture of heaven.**
6   **HUGH: Heaven? That doesn't look like heaven.**
7   **ARTIST: That's because I'm still creating it. You see these**
8   **clouds?**
9   **HUGH: Is that what they are?**
10   **ARTIST: Of course! Heaven is kind of a misty place, so I**
11   **included clouds.** *(Draws a road and gates.)*
12   **HUGH: I see. What are those straight lines right there?** *(BILLY*
13   *enters.)*
14   **ARTIST: I'm sure you've heard the typical tales about what**
15   **heaven might be like: pearly gates, streets of gold, and all**
16   **that.**
17   **HUGH: Of course.**
18   **ARTIST: So I've added the gates and road into my drawing.**
19   **Oh, I almost forgot to add this behind the gates.** *(Draws a*
20   *house.)*
21   **HUGH: A house?**
22   **ARTIST: Jesus said, "In my father's house are many mansions"**
23   *(John 14:2 KJV).* **And I'm going to add a little hill nearby.**
24   *(Draws a hill.)*
25   **HUGH: A cloudy hill, no doubt. Where's the grass?**
26   **ARTIST: There's no grass in heaven.**
27   **HUGH: The book of Revelation says God is going to make a**
28   **new heaven and a new earth, meaning good-bye, gold**
29   **streets, and hello, green grass.**
30   **ARTIST: That's not what it means. Hey, give me back my green**
31   **marker!**
32   **HUGH:** *(Takes the green marker or paint brush and dabs on some*
33   *green.)* **You need some color in this picture. Heaven is a**
34   **beautiful place! Don't make it so bland. You gotta use**
35   **more than two colors, like what you have here.**
36   **ARTIST:** *(Takes away the green.)* **That's because heaven is full of**

1   **light. It's so bright that it washes out the other colors.**

2   **HUGH: I think it's so bright that it *enhances* all the colors. Sort**

3   **of like how a rainbow enhances a cloud.** *(Picks up yellow*

4   *and red and starts to draw.)*

5   **ARTIST: Now see here, I'm the artist! Keep your paws off my**

6   **colors.**

7   **HUGH: I'm only adding a few minor improvements. You need**

8   **more red to show some battle scars.**

9   **ARTIST: Battle scars? Heaven is a peaceful place!** *(Tries to take*

10   *away the red marker, but HUGH fends him off.)*

11   **HUGH: It's peaceful enough now, but what happened at the**

12   **beginning of time when Lucifer was fighting Michael? It**

13   **was a war zone. Don't you think after one-third of the**

14   **angels fell, there would have been some sort of debris?**

15   **ARTIST: I don't care. I'm not adding debris.** *(Either erases the red,*

16   *or tries to cover it with some other color.)*

17   **HUGH:** *(Picks up some black.)* **Here, just a few swords —**

18   **ARTIST:** *(Grabs it.)* **Give that back to me!**

19   **HUGH: Come on, the pearly gate thing is corny. The most**

20   **important thing you want to show in heaven is the angels**

21   **ready for battle.** *(He reaches for another color. The ARTIST*

22   *slaps his hand.)*

23   **ARTIST: The most important thing in heaven is the Book of**

24   **Life. I'm going to draw that right here.**

25   **HUGH: You're going to ruin the picture.** *(He grabs another color,*

26   *but the ARTIST grabs his arm.)* **Let go of my arm!**

27   **ARTIST: Keep away from my drawing.**

28   **HUGH: I'm only trying to improve it for your own good.**

29   **ARTIST: My drawing doesn't need your help.**

30   **HUGH: It needs substance. I said, let go!**

31   **ARTIST: It needs serenity. Stop struggling and drop the**

32   **marker!** *(BILLY reaches over during their struggle and draws a*

33   *stick figure.)* **What are you drawing?**

34   **BILLY: Jesus. My daddy said the most important person in**

35   **heaven is Jesus.**

36   **HUGH:** *(Stops struggling with the ARTIST.)* **He's right.**

1   ARTIST: We were so busy focusing on the little unimportant
2   things that we forgot the main reason we're going to
3   heaven.
4   HUGH: Seems kind of silly now.
5   ARTIST: Sure does. Thanks, kid. *(He gathers his paints or markers*
6   *and exits.)*
7   BILLY: Wow. You guys fight like me and my friends.
8   HUGH: Welcome to the adult world, kid.

An Assessment of Prayer

Theme
Prayer

Scripture Reference
1 Thessalonians 5:18

Synopsis
A professor examines various types of table prayers, but the students have their own ideas about what prayer should be.

Cast
Professor
Student 1
Student 2
Student 3
Child 1
Child 2

Props
Whiteboard with pointer stick

Setting
A classroom. Each student will need a chair.

Note: This sketch can be increased up to a cast of nine or downsized to a cast of two, with one professor and one student asking all the questions.

1　(*PROFESSOR stands at whiteboard. STUDENTS 1-3 sit on*
2　*chairs at one side of the board.*)
3　PROFESSOR: Welcome, one and all. Today we will study
4　intently on the sanctity of prayer and the proper way to
5　speak to the Almighty. We start with the basic table
6　prayer. (*Points to the whiteboard.*)
7　Come Lord Jesus, be our guest,
8　And let these gifts to us be blessed. Amen.
9　Now, isn't that nice? Here, we are inviting Jesus to our
10　table to dine with us. Our food is our gift from God, so we
11　ask him to bless it. See how wonderfully simplistic this
12　is?
13　Now, our second table prayer is just as basic but a little
14　more mindful of others. (*Points to the board.*) "Bless us,
15　Lord, for these thy bountiful gifts." You see, again we
16　acknowledge the good Lord for our food and ask him to
17　bless it. We continue: "Help us to be mindful of all our
18　blessings and the needs of those who have less." Here we
19　also ask the Lord to help us remember our own blessings
20　and to be aware of others who need to be blessed as well.
21　So this sums up our talk on table prayers and their correct
22　usage.
23　STUDENT 1: (*Raises hand and steps out from the audience.*)
24　Professor? You forgot all the prayers from different
25　groups of people.
26　PROFESSOR: We won't be covering denominations in this
27　class.
28　STUDENT 1: No sir, I'm talking about *us*, the younger
29　generation. For example, what about the Superman
30　Prayer? It's a classic!
31　PROFESSOR: The what?
32　STUDENT 1: The Superman Prayer. It goes like this: (*Raises one*
33　*arm up in a fist, one arm down to his side: like Superman flying.*
34　*Other extras in the audience come up and join STUDENT 1 and*
35　*sing to the tune of the Superman theme song.*) We thank you,
36　God, for giving us food. (*Switch arms*) We thank you, God,

1 for giving us food. *(Both arms in the air, like Superman flying)*
2 For the food we eat, and the friends we meet, we thank
3 you, God, for giving us food.
4 PROFESSOR: Well, uh … it is original, I must say, but it leaves
5 out the blessing. You know that's very important with any
6 table prayer.
7 STUDENT 2: In that case, how about this one? *(STUDENT 2*
8 *starts the prayer and the rest join in to the tune of* The Addams
9 Family *theme song.)*
10 Do-do-do-do, *(Snap fingers twice)*
11 Do-do-do-do, *(Snap, snap)*
12 Do-do-do-do, do-do-do-do, do-do-do-do. *(Snap, snap)*
13 We thank you for our food, Lord,
14 And all the things you do, Lord.
15 We thank you for our food, Lord, and all our family.
16 Do-do-do-do, *(Snap, snap)* Do-do-do-do, *(Snap, snap)*
17 Do-do-do-do, do-do-do-do, do-do-do-do, Amen!
18 PROFESSOR: Well, that one added a bit more "thankfulness,"
19 but I'm not sure about the whole monster-tune-to-Jesus
20 thing.
21 STUDENT 3: *(Raises hand.)* Don't forget the redneck prayer.
22 PROFESSOR: Now see here, as Christians there should be no
23 class distinction between rich and poor, north and
24 south —
25 STUDENT 3: Rub-a-dub-dub, Thanks for the grub. Yeaaa, God!
26 PROFESSOR: I can guarantee that some of us will never go
27 near that prayer.
28 CHILD 1: Professor, you forgot the pre-K prayer.
29 PROFESSOR: The pre-K prayer?
30 CHILD 1: Bless 'em hot, bless 'em cold, bless what's in the pot,
31 nine days old.
32 PROFESSOR: Hmmmm. There are lots of blessings to that
33 prayer, but I'm not sure your mother will appreciate the
34 length of time her food has been sitting out.
35 CHILD 2: What about this one, Professor? *(Singing)*
36 "Thank you for the world so sweet,

1   Thank you for the food we eat,
2   Thank you for the birds that sing,
3   Thank you, God, for everything."
4   PROFESSOR: Now there's a song with lots of thankfulness in
5   it.
6   STUDENT 1: Don't forget the Speedo Prayer, Professor.
7   PROFESSOR: The Speedo Prayer?
8   STUDENT 2: Sure! It's used whenever you're in a hurry. *(This*
9   *prayer starts slow, then speeds up very fast.)*
10   Thank thee, Father, for this food,
11   *(Faster)* Best portion t' use,
12   *(Faster)* Feed our soul, better life,
13   *(Fastest)* Pardon our sins, heaven's sake, Amen.
14   PROFESSOR: *(Taken aback)* Well, uh, that certainly is fast all
15   right, and it's got soul in there ... someplace.
16   STUDENT 3: Then there's the drive-through prayer: Bless this
17   bunch as they munch their lunch.
18   PROFESSOR: I think the important point of this lesson can be
19   found in 1 Thessalonians 5:18: "In everything give
20   thanks, for this is the will of God." All supplications are
21   music to his ears, even if they are a bit off-key down here.

Babylonian Babble

Theme
Languages, the Tower of Babel

Scripture Reference
Genesis 11:1-9

Synopsis
A short commercial presents immense confusion.

Cast
Spokesperson (Male or female)

Costumes
Biblical clothing

Props
A coin purse and a "Tower of Babel" model
(Note: We just glued small boxes on top of larger ones.)

Setting
A television studio

1   *(SPOKESPERSON stands at Center Stage, addressing the*
2   *congregation.)*
3   SPOKESPERSON: Hello. Are you tired of being ordinary? Is
4   the light of hope flickering out? Then don't delay any
5   longer. You can be a contributing factor toward your own
6   salvation! That's right — for a small fee of three hundred
7   million drachmas, you can contribute to the Tower of
8   Babel Foundation. *(Holds up a picture or a model of the Tower*
9   *of Babel.)*
10   Be there to touch the sky and see God face to face. You
11   can be the first to say, "Yo, God, what's happening?"
12   Imagine being the envy of neighboring communities
13   when they see you commune with the Almighty as an
14   equal. Remember, you can only talk to God when you
15   contribute from your pocketbook. *(Holds up coin purse and*
16   *shakes it.)*
17   Pick up your quill right now and write to us. The
18   address is Tower of Babel ... yeh komi se dost ...
19   *(SPOKESPERSON speaks several sentences in a made-up*
20   *language. He/she is totally unaware of anything unusual*
21   *happening. He/she picks up the change purse, shakes it again,*
22   *then holds a pose and smiles while displaying the model of Babel.*
23   *Exaggerates his/her gestures while explaining the product in the*
24   *made-up language. SPOKESPERSON may conclude with a*
25   *freeze while smiling, or a fellow ACTOR may try to shoo the*
26   *SPOKESPERSON, and thus the commercial, off the stage. The*
27   *SPOKESPERSON is offended by this intrusion and argues in*
28   *gibberish with the interrupting ACTOR as they exit.)*

Campaign Promises

Theme
Hell, choices

Scripture Reference
John 3:19-21

Synopsis
A man stands between heaven and hell,
contemplating the best offer.

Cast
Satan
Doug
Angel 1
Angel 2
Extras for heaven and hell

Costumes
Angel and demon costumes. Choir robes work well for Angel
costumes. Red shirts may be worn for demon costumes.
The Extras may wear party hats.

Props
None

Setting
A location between heaven and hell

1   *(SATAN sees DOUG standing at Center Stage and approaches*
2   *him.)*
3   SATAN: Hello there. I see you're standing before the pearly
4   gates.
5   DOUG: Yeah, I'm getting ready to go in.
6   SATAN: And what do you know about this place, other than it
7   has a high vaulted entrance?
8   DOUG: Well ... I heard the streets are made of gold.
9   SATAN: Exactly! Do you realize what a waste of perfectly good
10   material that is?
11   DOUG: It does seem a little extravagant.
12   SATAN: Look around you. Do you see anyone you know?
13   DOUG: As a matter of fact, I don't.
14   SATAN: And do you know why that is?
15   DOUG: No, but I'm told it's all written in that book.
16   SATAN: Ah yes, old Saint Pete has quite a job checking the
17   status of its members and then judging if they're *worthy*
18   enough to enter. It all sounds a bit snobbish, if you ask
19   me. It isn't the type of group I perceived you to be with.
20   DOUG: What else is there?
21   SATAN: Ah, what else indeed. Come with me and I'll show
22   you. *(SATAN and DOUG cross over to the other side of the*
23   *stage. Several EXTRAS with party hats enter, whooping it up*
24   *and having a great time.)*
25   DOUG: Wow, what is this place?
26   SATAN: We call it paradise, but those jealous types up there
27   call it hell.
28   DOUG: This is hell? I thought it was supposed to be a horrible
29   place.
30   SATAN: Yes, sadly, most people think so. Look around you.
31   Where else can you party for all eternity? In fact, most of
32   your friends are here.
33   DOUG: Really? Ron Widdermeyer?
34   SATAN: Died of a drug overdose, if I remember. Yes, he's here,
35   and now he inhales all the smoke he wants.
36   DOUG: What about Stafford Ellison?

1 SATAN: Killed himself and thirty others by starting a fire in his
2   apartment. He's down the road hanging out in the lake.
3 DOUG: This is incredible.
4 SATAN: I seem to recall that during your lifetime, you said
5   you'd rather party in hell where all your friends are.
6 DOUG: I know! But I was speaking figuratively. I didn't think
7   it was real.
8 SATAN: We aim to deliver only the best. Are you ready to join
9   us?
10 DOUG: I'm not sure. I'd like to check out heaven first.
11 SATAN: Suit yourself. *(SATAN exits. DOUG walks across the stage.*
12   *A group of ANGELS walks out, laughing and talking among*
13   *themselves. Others are praying, and two are listening to*
14   *something down below.)*
15 ANGEL 1: Did he say, "Bless and dare"?
16 ANGEL 2: Bear. Bless the bear! He's praying about his toy.
17 DOUG: Sounds like a waste of a prayer to me.
18 ANGEL 2: What else do you expect of a four-year-old?
19 ANGEL 1: Hey, it's time for our daily songfest. Want to join us?
20 DOUG: Thanks, but I'll pass.
21 ANGEL 1: Really? I've never met anyone who didn't want to go
22   before.
23 DOUG: I'm not much into singing.
24 ANGEL 2: Oh, there's much more to it than that. There's lots of
25   praising and hugging and spending time with loved ones.
26   It's really fun.
27 DOUG: Thanks, but I'm outta here. *(ANGELS exit as he crosses*
28   *over to the other side of the stage. SATAN enters.)* I can't stand
29   that place. It's way too bright. I want to join your group.
30 SATAN: Come on in. *(Quickly)* Slave, shut the gate.
31 DOUG: Hey, wait a minute — why is it so hot in here? Where
32   are all the people laughing and having a good time?
33   Where's the party?
34 SATAN: Oh, that. The campaign's over. Welcome to reality.

Counselor Judy

Theme
Prayer

Scripture Reference
Matthew 7:3-4; James 5:16

Synopsis
A bitter Pastor reaches out to Judy for advice.

Cast
Judy
Pastor

Props
A nail file

Setting
Judy's office.

1   *(JUDY is standing at Center Stage, filing her nails. She always*
2   *responds in a deadpan monotone, with no emotion in her voice.*
3   *Another description is "sheer boredom." The PASTOR enters.)*
4   PASTOR: Judy, I have a problem that only you can help me
5   with.
6   JUDY: *(Doesn't look up from her filing.)*That's understandable.
7   PASTOR: However, I must ask for your complete confidence in
8   this.
9   JUDY: Having trouble with your congregation again?
10   PASTOR: They're driving me nuts! They argue over every little
11   thing, they demand every moment of my time, and
12   speaking of time, they've taken to clocking my sermons.
13   Can you believe they actually clear their throats when I go
14   over twenty minutes?
15   JUDY: Have you tried locking your office?
16   PASTOR: Of course.
17   JUDY: What about ignoring their phone calls?
18   PASTOR: I've done that too. You have no idea how hostile it
19   made them.
20   JUDY: I can imagine.
21   PASTOR: Somehow, they always seem to find me. You know,
22   I'd be a really great pastor if it wasn't for my congregation.
23   JUDY: I'm sure your wife would disagree.
24   PASTOR: You're probably right; she disagrees over everything
25   I say. Come to think of it, I'd be a really great husband if
26   it wasn't for my wife.
27   JUDY: And a really great father, if it wasn't for your children.
28   PASTOR: You see what I'm up against? I knew you'd
29   understand, Judy.
30   JUDY: More than you know. Have you tried prayer?
31   PASTOR: *(Indignant)* Judy, please! It's my job to pray for
32   people. I pray for their crummy attitudes, their rebellious
33   natures, their obstinate stubbornness ...
34   JUDY: Have you tried praying *with* them?
35   PASTOR: With them? You mean together?
36   JUDY: Scripture does say that "when two or more are gathered

1 in prayer, Jesus is among them" *(Matthew 18-20 KJV)*.
2 PASTOR: Of course I know that! But I prefer to pray for them
3 in solitude and leave the generic prayers out in the open.
4 JUDY: Prayer draws people together. It creates a oneness
5 among all members. Besides, once they see your attitude
6 changing with prayer, they will often respond in kind.
7 PASTOR: There's nothing wrong with my attitude.
8 JUDY: Splinter in the eye, Pastor.
9 PASTOR: You're saying that I'm concentrating so much on
10 their faults that I can't see the faults in myself?
11 JUDY: Jesus does say that before you can remove the splinter
12 from your neighbor's eye, you must remove the beam
13 from your own.
14 PASTOR: But I can't admit my faults. They might view me as
15 weak!
16 JUDY: We are all weak. It is Christ who makes us strong.
17 PASTOR: Strong in *him*.
18 JUDY: Touché.
19 PASTOR: Then I'll go pray with them. I think I'll even do it out
20 loud this time. *(Mumbles.)* Although they'll probably
21 criticize how I do it.
22 JUDY: Prayer sometimes takes one splinter at a time.

Double Jeopardy

Theme
Salvation through grace

Scripture Reference
John 3:18-21; Galatians 3:10-14, 1 John 2:1-2,
Exodus 20:5, Deuteronomy 27:26

Synopsis
A group of newly arrived angels are in shock when
they learn the requirement for entering heaven.

Cast
Judge
Prosecutor
Jesus
Barb
Martin
Claire

Costumes
Judge costume (a choir robe works well); Prosecutor wears
a suit (white is nice but any color is fine); Jesus wears a
biblical robe; and the defendants wear normal clothing.

Props
Gavel (optional)

Setting
Heaven. Use the pulpit or a table and chair positioned
higher than the other actors for the Judge's bench.

1 (CLAIRE, BARB, MARTIN, and PROSECUTOR are in place
2 with the JUDGE sitting at his bench.
3 CLAIRE: Wow, this is incredible! Are we really in heaven?
4 BARB: Of course we are. Look at the pearly gates.
5 MARTIN: And the streets of gold! And all this time I thought
6   the Bible was just stating it figuratively.
7 CLAIRE: Look — there's an angel.
8 PROSECUTOR: Hold it right there, please.
9 BARB: My name is Barb, and these are my good friends, Claire
10   and Martin.
11 MARTIN: We were in a car accident together.
12 CLAIRE: Took us right out. No time for last-minute
13   confessions.
14 PROSECUTOR: *(Unimpressed)* Uh-huh. *(Turns toward the*
15   *JUDGE.)* The accused is here to see you, Your Honor.
16 JUDGE: Bring them forward.
17 BARB: I don't get it.
18 MARTIN: What are we accused of?
19 CLAIRE: Surely there are worse people than us.
20 JUDGE: Silence! Mr. Prosecutor, you will read the charges.
21 PROSECUTOR: Yes, Your Honor. The defendants are accused
22   of breaking every single commandment and failing to
23   live a holy life.
24 BARB: We did the best we could.
25 MARTIN: We're only human after all.
26 JUDGE: There will be no outburst in my court. How do you
27   plead?
28 CLAIRE: Plead? Don't we get a trial?
29 PROSECUTOR: Your "trial" was your life, and you failed
30   miserably.
31 MARTIN: How did we fail?
32 PROSECUTOR: You failed to honor your father and mother.
33 MARTIN: They died when I was a teenager.
34 PROSECUTOR: You were very rebellious at the time.
35 MARTIN: Most teenagers are. I didn't think you would hold it
36   over my head my entire life!

1   JUDGE: Silence! No excuses.
2   CLAIRE: *(To MARTIN)* **Tough crowd.**
3   JUDGE: *(To PROSECUTOR, while pointing at CLAIRE)* **Tell that**
4   *thief* **this will be the last time she speaks out of turn in my**
5   **court.**
6   CLAIRE: Thief? I never stole anything.
7   PROSECUTOR: You often took pencils from work, and once
8   you even took home a pen.
9   CLAIRE: Pens? Are you kidding me?
10   PROSECUTOR: By doing so, you broke the eighth
11   commandment.
12   CLAIRE: That's ridiculous! It's not like I stole a car or
13   embezzled millions of dollars.
14   JUDGE: I do not make concessions concerning the size of the
15   article. You are guilty!
16   CLAIRE: Guilty? I'm guilty?
17   BARB: Tough break, Claire.
18   JUDGE: *(To BARB)* **So are you.**
19   BARB: What did I do?
20   PROSECUTOR: You broke the fourth commandment to
21   remember the Sabbath day and keep it holy.
22   BARB: Without clear instruction, that commandment is a little
23   vague.
24   PROSECUTOR: It doesn't matter. One slip of any
25   commandment makes you guilty of all ten.
26   CLAIRE: But that's not fair!
27   MARTIN: Who made up these rules, anyway?
28   PROSECUTOR: The judge.
29   JUDGE: And as the judge, I pronounce you all guilty! Guilty of
30   living a less than perfect life.
31   PROSECUTOR: And since perfect people are the only ones
32   allowed in heaven, you will have to go to that other place.
33   MARTIN: Wait a minute. Don't we get some sort of
34   representation?
35   JUDGE: *(To PROSECUTOR)* **Do we have anyone?**
36   PROSECUTOR: Who would want them?

1 JESUS: *(Entering)* I would.
2 BARB: It's Jesus!
3 CLAIRE: We're saved!
4 JUDGE: You plan to speak on behalf of these low-lifers?
5 JESUS: I do, Your Honor.
6 JUDGE: They are filthy, horrible sinners.
7 JESUS: That they are, Your Honor.
8 MARTIN: Hey, I thought he was on our side.
9 JUDGE: They ruined relationships and did their own thing!
10 JESUS: Yes, they did. Pretty tacky, isn't it?
11 BARB: You're not supposed to agree.
12 JUDGE: They don't deserve to go to heaven.
13 JESUS: No, they don't.
14 CLAIRE: We're doomed.
15 JUDGE: So my sentence for them is to spend the rest of eternity
16   in a place where boiling lakes reside.
17 CLAIRE: You know, I'm not really the outdoorsy type.
18 JESUS: Hold on, Judge. You have no jurisdiction to sentence
19   these people.
20 JUDGE: What?
21 JESUS: I've already paid the price for these people. My own
22   blood wiped out their sins.
23 MARTIN: *(Pats JESUS on the back.)* Good boy. You tell him.
24 JESUS: *(To the GROUP)* Quick, get behind me. *(BARB, CLAIRE,*
25   *and MARTIN line up single file behind JESUS.)* From now on,
26   Your Honor, when you look at these defendants, you will
27   see me instead.
28 JUDGE: They do suddenly appear a lot cleaner.
29 PROSECUTOR: But they've already been judged!
30 JESUS: You can't sentence someone twice for the same offense.
31   It's called "double jeopardy."
32 BARB: Yes. *(Points at JESUS.)* What he said.
33 JESUS: The sentence has already been carried out. The price
34   has been paid.When you look at these people now, Your
35   Honor, what do you see?
36 JUDGE: I see you. They are perfect in every way.

1   PROSECUTOR: But Your Honor —
2   JUDGE: Pass into the kingdom of heaven.
3   BARB: Thank you, Jesus.
4   MARTIN: *(Points to JESUS.)* You the man!
5   CLAIRE: I wasn't worried a bit. *(BARB, MARTIN, and CLAIRE*
6   *exit.)*
7   JUDGE: *(To PROSECUTOR)* Who do we have next on our roster?
8   PROSECUTOR: Fifty million people, all wanting Jesus to
9   represent them.
10   JUDGE: This could take a while. Next! *(ALL exit.)*

Eagles' Wings

Theme
Faith, obedience

Scripture Reference
Deuteronomy 32:11; Isaiah 40:31

Synopsis
One soldier finds it difficult to take a leap of faith.

Cast
Commander
Josh
Ray
Dirk

Props
Army helmets (or bicycle helmets) and backpacks.

Setting
Imagine an airplane with super soldiers ready to jump.
Position four chairs to stand on (two rows of two).

Note: The noise is loud, so the soldiers speak as though they
are *shouting*. Optional sound effect of wind.

1   *(COMMANDER, JOSH, RAY, and DIRK each stand on a chair,*
2   *as if in an airplane and ready to jump.)*
3   COMMANDER: This is it, guys — the leap of faith. Is everyone
4   ready?
5   JOSH: Ready, sir!
6   RAY: Ready, sir! *(They pause and look at DIRK, who says nothing.)*
7   COMMANDER: I said, is everyone ready?
8   JOSH: Ready, sir!
9   RAY: I'm ready, sir! *(Pause as they all look at DIRK.)*
10   DIRK: Oh no, no, no, you're not getting me to jump.
11   COMMANDER: It's not a jump; it's a leap of faith.
12   DIRK: Yeah, well, whatever you call it, I'm not doing it.
13   COMMANDER: Look, Private — for whatever it's worth,
14   you've all been called to take this leap.
15   DIRK: I never received the phone call, sir.
16   COMMANDER: The calling came from God. You received it in
17   your heart.
18   DIRK: That's a very shallow place for me, sir.
19   JOSH: I can vouch for him, sir.
20   RAY: He's extremely shallow, sir.
21   COMMANDER: Private, it's not for me to decide how
22   dysfunctional a person's character is. When the Lord calls
23   us to faith, we leap.
24   DIRK: It's a trick. I know how this works. I jump, and the three
25   of you watch me fall and land on my face.
26   JOSH: I sure would like to see that, sir.
27   RAY: That would be extremely funny, sir.
28   COMMANDER: Private, don't you know what it says in
29   Deuteronomy 32:11?
30   DIRK: That wasn't required reading before the trip, sir.
31   COMMANDER: It says, "He was like an eagle building its nest
32   that flutters over its young. It spreads its wings to catch
33   them, and carries them on its feathers."
34   DIRK: What does that mean, sir?
35   COMMANDER: When a baby eagle leaps out of the nest, the
36   mother will fly directly underneath, helping it to learn to

1   spread its wings and preventing the baby from falling.
2   DIRK: What does that have to do with me, sir?
3   COMMANDER: It means God will fly with us. His wing will
4   guide our destination, support us when we feel tired or
5   frightened, and lift us up when we're discouraged.
6   DIRK: So we're never alone, sir?
7   COMMANDER: That's right, Private. So, is everyone ready?
8   JOSH: I'm ready, sir!
9   COMMANDER: Then go! *(JOSH jumps down, raises his arms in*
10   *victory, and exits.)*
11 RAY: I'm ready, sir!
12 COMMANDER: Then go! *(RAY jumps down, raises his arms in*
13   *victory, and exits.)*
14 DIRK: *(Looks down and shakes his head.)* Oh, no, no, no. I don't
15   think so.
16 COMMANDER: Dirk, the Lord is calling, I command you to
17   leap.
18 DIRK: Sorry, wrong number. Try again when we're closer to the
19   ground.
20 COMMANDER: *(Points down.)* Look, an eagle!
21 DIRK: Where? *(The COMMANDER pushes DIRK off the chair. He*
22   *lands and looks around, stunned.)*
23 COMMANDER: *(To audience)* Sometimes a leap of faith
24   requires a little push.
25 DIRK: This isn't so bad. *(Shouts up to COMMANDER.)* I told
26   you I could do this. I'm an eagle that can walk the walk
27   and talk the talk. Yes sir, I have enough faith to move
28   mountains! *(DIRK exits.)*
29 COMMANDER: *(To audience)* And sometimes the leap of faith
30   requires short-term memory loss. *(COMMANDER jumps*
31   *and exits.)*

Fix-it Man

Theme
Surrendering, the cross.

Scripture Reference
Mark 16:24; Hebrews 12:2

Synopsis
Got a broken life? Call on the carpenters.

Cast
Redmond
Smith
Piccoli

Costumes
Work clothes for all.

Props
Toolbox with glue, thumbtacks, a hammer, and pliers,
plus a large assortment of broken wood.

Setting
A construction site. There is a large cross at
the side of the stage.

1 *(SMITH enters. He sees RICHMOND looking over a pile of wood*
2 *jumbled together in a pile at Center Stage.)*
3 SMITH: Hey, Richmond — what are you doing?
4 RICHMOND: Uh, I don't quite know.
5 SMITH: Oh man, what is this?
6 RICHMOND: My life.
7 SMITH: Your life? How did this happen?
8 RICHMOND: I don't know. I just, like, woke up and
9 everything was a mess. I mean, look at this split wood.
10 *(Picks up some wood and shows it to him.)* That's the last of my
11 parents' relationship. It's, like, totally ruined.
12 SMITH: Bummer.
13 RICHMOND: *(Picks up another piece of wood.)* And look at this,
14 dude. My girlfriend and I are totally broken in half.
15 SMITH: That looks permanent.
16 RICHMOND: And I can't even begin to sort out this mess.
17 SMITH: Is that your entire high school experience?
18 RICHMOND: What's left of it.
19 SMITH: That's pretty gnarly.
20 RICHMOND: Tell me about it. *(PICCOLI enters, holding up a*
21 *bottle of glue.)*
22 PICCOLI: Richmond, I got it.
23 SMITH: What is it?
24 PICCOLI: Wood glue. We're going to fix Richmond's life.
25 SMITH: You can't fix Richmond's life, Piccoli.
26 PICCOLI: Sure I can. My dad is a washer repairman. He has
27 some awesome tools!
28 SMITH: *(Picks up two pieces of wood.)* This is totally broken.
29 Wood glue won't touch this.
30 PICCOLI: I can fix it! *(He takes the wood and tries to glue it*
31 *together.)* You got any string?
32 RICHMOND: No. All I've got are a few thumbtacks.
33 PICCOLI: Perfect. Let me have them. *(Takes the tacks and tries to*
34 *dig them into the wood.)*
35 RICHMOND: I don't think that's going to work.
36 PICCOLI: I'm serious. I can fix this! *(The wood doesn't hold and*

1   *breaks in half again.)* **I think this wood is defective, dude.**

2   RICHMOND: **It's beyond repair. There's no hope.**

3   PICCOLI: **Never say die, dude.** Here — **gimme that hammer.**

4   **We'll force it together by sheer brute strength.** *(Tries to*

5   *hammer one end on to the other.)*

6   SMITH: **You know, Richmond, your life isn't hopeless.**

7   RICHMOND: **I don't know about you, but this tangled,**

8   **jumbled-up pile of my life seems pretty hopeless to me.**

9   SMITH: **I was once like you. My life was falling apart around**

10   **me, but I found the One who can truly help me.**

11   RICHMOND: **Who is that?**

12   SMITH: **The best repairman in the whole world. The Jewish**

13   **carpenter.**

14   RICHMOND: **I don't know, man. I don't think I'm ready to**

15   **give up control.**

16   SMITH: **Control of what?**

17   RICHMOND: **You know ...** *(Picks up a broken piece of wood.)* **All of**

18   **this!**

19   PICCOLI: *(Grabs the wood from RICHMOND.)* **I can fix this, too.**

20   **My dad has a whole set of power tools.**

21   RICHMOND: **What's so great about the Jewish carpenter?**

22   SMITH: **You have to go to the cross to find out.**

23   RICHMOND: **The cross?**

24   SMITH: **The place where Christ was crucified. When you kneel**

25   **at the cross and give him your life, his blood washes you**

26   **clean and makes you whole again.**

27   RICHMOND: **What kind of magic is that?**

28   SMITH: **It's not magic. It's a surrender.**

29   PICCOLI: *(Examining two pieces of wood)* **I don't know, man. I**

30   **think this dude may need a bit of magic to fix up these**

31   **pieces.**

32   RICHMOND: **So do I take these to him?**

33   SMITH: **That's right. And trust him to fix it, because he's the**

34   **carpenter.**

35   PICCOLI: **Hey, I'm not doing such a bad job here.** *(He waves two*

36   *pieces of wood badly stuck together that immediately become*

1   *disconnected and fall to the ground.)*
2   **RICHMOND: Give me my life, Piccoli.** *(He takes the wood out of*
3   *PICCOLI's hand and gathers the rest.)*
4   **PICCOLI: Aw, come on, man. I can fix this. Look, I've got my**
5   **dad's pliers.**
6   **RICHMOND:** *(Takes the pieces to the cross and lays them at its base.*
7   *He lifts his hands in the air.)* **I surrender.**

Fourth Down, Eternity to Go

Theme
Perseverance (And a great choice for Superbowl Sunday!)

Scripture Reference
1 Corinthians 9:24-27; Philippians 3:12-14

Synopsis
A player learns the value of staying in the game.

Cast
Coach
Assistant Coach
Bertinelli
Extras are optional. You may simulate the Coach
motioning the players to go in instead.

Costumes
Football jerseys.

Props
Headset microphones for coaches.

Setting
A football field.

1   *(Scene starts with the COACH, ASSISTANT COACH, and*
2   *BERTINELLI standing on the sidelines. When they watch the*
3   *game, they look out over the heads of the congregation.)*
4   ASSISTANT COACH: The game's not looking so good, Coach.
5   COACH: I agree. We need a new game plan. Bertinelli!
6   BERTINELLI: *(Snaps to attention.)* Yeah, Coach?
7   COACH: Get in there and tell them to run a three-man
8   formation, four wide. Got it?
9   BERTINELLI: Got it, Coach. *(BERTINELLI exits. Pause as*
10   *COACHES watch the play.)*
11   ASSISTANT COACH: Yes! That worked real well. We needed
12   that first down.
13   COACH: Right. For the next play, tell them to give it to Jackson
14   up the middle.
15   ASSISTANT COACH: *(Speaks into his mouthpiece.)* Jackson, up
16   the middle. *(Pauses, as if watching the play.)*
17   COACH: Ah, only five yards. Tell them to do an away pass to
18   Rodriguez.
19   ASSISTANT COACH: *(Speaking into his mouthpiece)* Yes, short
20   pass to Rodriguez. *(Pause)* No, we don't want to run again.
21   *(Looks up to watch the play.)* Incomplete. That makes it third
22   down.
23   COACH: Let's go four wide again.
24   ASSISTANT COACH: Four wide. Look for Taylor downfield.
25   *(Pause)* No, we don't want to run it again. *(Pause)* No, we're
26   not going to run a trick play. It's only third down, for
27   heaven's sake. Who's trying to call these plays?
28   COACH: Time-out.
29   ASSISTANT COACH: Time-out. Everyone take a knee.
30   *(BERTINELLI enters.)*
31   COACH: Bertinelli, what is going on out there?
32   BERTINELLI: They're on to us, Coach. They seem to sense
33   what we're about to do.
34   COACH: Two stopped plays do not constitute a "sense,"
35   Bertinelli. Tell them to run the plays I send in — no
36   exceptions.

1   BERTINELLI: OK, Coach. *(BERTINELLI exits.)*
2   ASSISTANT COACH: Greene is fading back. Oh no, they're
3   chasing him all over the field.
4   COACH: I see Taylor in the open. Throw it, throw it! *(Pause)* Yes!
5   ASSISTANT COACH: For a minute I thought they were going
6   to sack our quarterback.
7   COACH: All right, now let's hit them up the middle this time.
8   ASSISTANT COACH: *(Talking into his mouthpiece)* Jackson, up
9   the middle. *(Pause)* Tell Bertinelli I don't care what he
10   thinks! Run the play as ordered.
11   COACH: Tell Bertinelli to get off the field!
12   ASSISTANT COACH: Hang on, Connor is coming in for
13   Bertinelli. *(Motions for a player to go in. BERTINELLI enters.)*
14   BERTINELLI: Yeah, Coach?
15   COACH: Bertinelli, what in the world are you doing?
16   BERTINELLI: It's no good, Coach. They're harassing us out there.
17   COACH: Harassing?
18   BERTINELLI: Yeah. They're saying stuff like, "You're a mama's
19   boy," or "Your daddy never loved you," and "You'll never
20   be cool." Things like that.
21   COACH: Ignore the bullying, and concentrate on the job at
22   hand.
23   BERTINELLI: But it hurts our feelings, Coach.
24   COACH: Look, Bertinelli — when you chose to play on this
25   team, you had to know that meant others would criticize
26   you and even call you a wimp. But you've got to
27   remember that you're on the winning team. They are the
28   ones who are going to lose in the end. Now, get in there
29   and play the game.
30   BERTINELLI: OK, Coach. *(BERTINELLI exits.)*
31   ASSISTANT COACH: This is looking good. We've got the ball
32   on the ten-yard line and —
33   COACH and ASSISTANT COACH: *(Together)* No!
34   COACH: Fumble. I can't look.
35   ASSISTANT COACH: They got the ball.
36   COACH: We were so close, too. OK, send in the defense.

1 (*ASSISTANT COACH motions for PLAYERS to go in.*
2 *BERTINELLI enters.*)
3 BERTINELLI: Sorry, Coach. I let that big fella slip past me. I
4 don't know what happened.
5 COACH: Mistakes happen, Bertinelli. Just be ready to go in
6 again.
7 BERTINELLI: You mean the game's not over?
8 COACH: It's just a fumble. We just need to hold them off and
9 we're back in the game.
10 BERTINELLI: But we failed. Shouldn't we quit while we're
11 ahead?
12 COACH: Quit? We never quit. We pick ourselves up and keep
13 going.
14 BERTINELLI: But what if I fail again?
15 COACH: You pick yourself up again.
16 BERTINELLI: How long do I have to do that, Coach?
17 COACH: Until the day you die.
18 BERTINELLI: Then what happens after I die?
19 COACH: Then you win.
20 BERTINELLI: I win? It sounds more like I lose.
21 COACH: You're missing the big picture. Once you go to
22 heaven, you get to play with the greatest quarterback that
23 ever lived.
24 BERTINELLI: Who's that?
25 COACH: Jesus.
26 BERTINELLI: Wow. I actually get to play on the same team as
27 Jesus?
28 COACH: For all of eternity.
29 BERTINELLI: What's his team's name?
30 COACH: The Saints, of course.
31 BERTINELLI: Cool.
32 ASSISTANT COACH: We got the ball again, Coach.
33 COACH: Good. Bertinelli, get in there and fight, and don't
34 forget —
35 BERTINELLI: I know, I know. Don't be afraid because we're on
36 the winning team. (*ALL exit.*)

Front Lines

Theme
Spiritual warfare, good works

Scripture Reference
2 Timothy 2:3-4

Synopsis
The battle is raging. The front lines face hardships while those away from the battle complain about the conditions.

Cast
Michael
Gabriel
Amos
Malcolm
Haddai
Extras for Michael's army and the Enemy's army

Costumes
Michael's army is dressed in white and the Enemy's army is dressed in red.

Props
Plastic or cardboard swords, Nerf swords, or anything soft; microphone headsets or walkie-talkies

Setting
A spiritual battlefield. You will need some sort of barrier, which may be as simple as a table turned over on its side.

1   *(The scene begins with MICHAEL and AMOS behind a small*
2   *barrier with several EXTRAS on each side. MICHAEL speaks*
3   *into his walkie-talkie.)*
4   MICHAEL: Gabriel, we've secured sector one. What is your
5   position?
6   GABRIEL: *(Voiced Off-stage)* We're lining up in sector two. We
7   got a fix on Charlie's position. Do you copy?
8   MICHAEL: Copy that. You've got clearance; notify me when
9   you're ready.
10   GABRIEL: *(Voiced Off-stage)* Copy that. Over and out.
11   AMOS: Everyone's secured, Michael. Do you see them yet?
12   MICHAEL: Not yet, but I know they're close.
13   AMOS: How do you know?
14   MICHAEL: Ten thousand years of battle. I can smell them out.
15   AMOS: Your instincts must be pretty good, because they're
16   right behind us! *(The ENEMY enters. The ANGELS turn and*
17   *engage in battle. MICHAEL steps forward and speaks into his*
18   *walkie-talkie.)*
19   MICHAEL: Gabriel, Gabriel, we're under enemy attack.
20   Repeat, we are under enemy attack. Send all troops to this
21   sector. *(GABRIEL and his ARMY attack from Stage Right. They*
22   *chase the ENEMY Off-stage. All EXTRAS follow and exit,*
23   *leaving MICHAEL and GABRIEL at Center Stage.)*
24   MICHAEL: Well done, Gabriel. I knew you'd come through.
25   GABRIEL: We're comrades in arms, are we not?
26   MICHAEL: To the end of eternity.
27   GABRIEL: Whenever that is.
28   MICHAEL: How are your men?
29   GABRIEL: Exhausted, worn out, but ready to move on a
30   moment's notice.
31   MICHAEL: Good. We need to pursue these attackers. They're a
32   menace.
33   GABRIEL: We're ready.
34   MICHAEL: Let's go, then. This way. *(Both exit Stage Left just as*
35   *MALCOLM and HADDAI enters Stage Right. Malcolm is*
36   *leading the CASUALTIES.)*

1   MALCOLM: This way, people. The first aid station is just
2   ahead. *(He points toward Stage Left. The CASUALTIES hobble*
3   *toward the exit.)*
4   HADDAI: More wounded? Now we're going to have to cancel
5   our nightly sing-along. What happened?
6   MALCOLM: Michael's troops were attacked. Gabriel had to
7   rescue him.
8   HADDAI: What were they doing on the front lines? Don't they
9   know it's safer to hide in the brush a few million
10   kilometers away?
11   MALCOLM: The only problem with that tactic is that the
12   enemy gains ground.
13   HADDAI: Then they should retreat farther. I mean, this isn't
14   rocket science here.
15   MALCOLM: What's for supper?
16   HADDAI: Century-old fish.
17   MALCOLM: Again? We've had that for the last one hundred
18   years!
19   HADDAI: Well, if Michael and Gabriel would stop fighting
20   long enough to get us more food, we'd be eating better.
21   MALCOLM: But they never stop fighting.
22   HADDAI: You see the problem I have?
23   MALCOLM: How much longer can we live under these
24   hardships? *(MALCOLM and HADDAI exit just as MICHAEL*
25   *and GABRIEL enter.)*
26   MICHAEL: How much longer can you live under these
27   hardships?
28   GABRIEL: Whatever it takes. You know my troops and I are
29   ready for battle at your command.
30   MICHAEL: It could be a long time before we get any rest or
31   nourishment.
32   GABRIEL: *(Shrugs.)* Food is overrated. Besides, we fight for the
33   Lord, do we not?
34   MICHAEL: Of course.
35   GABRIEL: And the saints down on earth need protection,
36   right?

1   MICHAEL: Constant protection.
2   GABRIEL: Well then, until the final battle, let us not grow
3   weary of doing good.
4   MICHAEL: Let us do all we can to stand. *(Both exit.)*

The Gift

Theme
Gifts of the Holy Spirit

Scripture Reference
1 Corinthians 12:1-11; Ephesians 4:7

Synopsis
A woman compares her gift to others'
with unsatisfactory results.

Cast
Salesman
Iris
Jade
Kat
Lilly

Costumes
Kat is dressed in an all-pink outfit.

Props
You will need several packages of various sizes and colors,
including one small package decorated in shiny paper and
bow, one bright pink package with pink ribbon and bow,
and one very large package, plus extra packages which
will be on the table for show. You'll also need a large
purse or handbag for Iris.

Setting
A retail outlet. Place a table at Center Stage,
with a sign saying "Free Gift."

1   *(The scene begins with the SALESMAN standing behind a table*
2   *of several beautifully wrapped gifts. IRIS enters.)*
3   **SALESMAN: Welcome, one and all. Gather 'round my table.**
4   **Everyone here receives a free gift. Come ... come.** *(IRIS,*
5   *JADE, KAT, and LILLY enter.)*
6   **IRIS: Oh, do I get a free gift?**
7   **SALESMAN: Are you a believer?**
8   **IRIS: I am.**
9   **SALESMAN: Then I have a gift for you — a special gift from**
10   **the Holy Spirit.**
11   **IRIS: I'm so excited!** *(SALESMAN hands her a small gift from the*
12   *table.)* **Oh, it's so beautiful! I especially love the pretty bow**
13   **and the shiny paper.**
14   **SALESMAN: And it's made especially for you.**
15   **IRIS: Really?**
16   **SALESMAN: Absolutely. Your personality, your interests, your**
17   **"being" as it were, all were taken into consideration when**
18   **your gift was prepared for you.**
19   **IRIS: Oh, thank you! Thank you so much.**
20   **JADE: Do you have a gift for me?**
21   **SALESMAN: Of course.** *(Hands her a large package.)*
22   **JADE: It's awesome!**
23   **SALESMAN: And made especially for you.** *(JADE exits.)*
24   **IRIS: Excuse me, but why is her gift bigger?**
25   **SALESMAN: I beg your pardon?**
26   **IRIS: Her gift. It's larger than mine. Why can't I have a big gift**
27   **like she has?**
28   **SALESMAN:** *(Looks confused.)* **Because that is her gift, and you**
29   **have your gift.**
30   **KAT: Do you have a gift for me?**
31   **SALESMAN: Of course I do.** *(Hands her a pink gift with a bright*
32   *pink bow)*
33   **KAT: Oh, it's so wonderful, and it is so *me*!**
34   **SALESMAN: It does seem to suit you.**
35   **IRIS: I like pink. Why didn't I get a pink one?**
36   **KAT: I can't wait to show all the girls!** *(KAT exits.)*

1   LILLY: Do you have a gift for me?

2   SALESMAN: I have several gifts for you.

3   IRIS: Several?! *(SALESMAN hands her three large presents. IRIS*

4   *stands there gaping at the gifts.)*

5   LILLY: Wow. This is intense.

6   SALESMAN: And it's a great responsibility to care for your

7   gifts.

8   LILLY: Not a problem. I'm an awesome multitasker.

9   SALESMAN: Of course you are. You would not have received

10   these gifts if we didn't think you could handle them.

11   *(LILLY exits.)*

12   IRIS: I'd like another gift.

13   SALESMAN: You have already received your gift.

14   IRIS: But why can't I have two gifts?

15   SALESMAN: Because that is what you received.

16   IRIS: In that case, then I would like to exchange this gift.

17   SALESMAN: Excuse me?

18   IRIS: I want to trade it in for another gift. How about that big

19   white one with the blue bow?

20   SALESMAN: I'm sorry, ma'am, but there are no exchanges.

21   IRIS: That's absurd. Why can't I have what the others have?

22   SALESMAN: Because the other gifts were not made with you

23   in mind.

24   IRIS: But I can do many more important things with a larger

25   and prettier gift. People will hardly notice if I carry

26   around this little thing.

27   SALESMAN: There is no value in the size or the amount of the

28   gift. All are considered equally important in the kingdom

29   of God.

30   IRIS: If you don't give me something else, I'm going to throw

31   away this gift.

32   SALESMAN: Sadly, you have that option. But you will not

33   receive another gift.

34   IRIS: But that's unfair! Well, I know what I'm going to do, then.

35   I'll stuff it in my bag so no one can see it and I won't be

36   embarrassed by it.

1   SALESMAN: I guarantee you will not be fulfilled by hiding
2   your gift, and you will not be as effective in your service
3   to the Lord.
4   IRIS: We'll see about that. *(JADE, KAT, and LILLY enter, still*
5   *holding their gifts.)*
6   JADE: Iris, are you still here?
7   KAT: We've been showing everyone our gifts.
8   LILLY: Aren't they wonderful? Where's yours?
9   IRIS: Oh ... uh, they made a mistake. My gift wasn't that little
10   old thing.
11   JADE: I thought it was beautiful.
12   KAT: And it was so shiny.
13   IRIS: It was, but ... um, my other gift was so big that they
14   shipped it to my house.
15   LILLY: Let's go see it!
16   IRIS: No! *(Quickly)* I mean, I don't want the rest of you to feel
17   bad when you see how big it is.
18   JADE: *(Looks out toward the audience.)* Hey, look! They all have
19   gifts, too!
20   KAT: There's so many of them.
21   LILLY: Let's go fellowship with them.
22   JADE and KAT: *(Ad-lib)* All right, let's do it, let's go.
23   IRIS: *(Sighs and begins to walk Off-stage. She suddenly stops, reaches*
24   *in her bag, and pulls out the small gift.)* Wait a minute,
25   everyone! I have a gift too. Look how beautiful it is! *(IRIS*
26   *runs Off-stage.)*

Give Up This Day
Our Daily Jelly Bread

Theme
Lenten season, giving

Scripture Reference
2 Corinthians 9:7

Synopsis
Four children experience the "hardship" of giving something up for Jesus during Lent.

Cast
(Names and gender may be changed)
Sarah
Peyton
Jordan
Taylor

Props
None

Setting
Nonspecific

1   *(TAYLOR and JORDAN enter, each holding on to PEYTON,*
2   *who can barely stand.)*
3   TAYLOR: *(Exhausted)* I ... can't ... go on.
4   JORDAN: Come on, Taylor. We've got to make it.
5   TAYLOR: I'm just too weak. I need food!
6   JORDAN: Peyton, stand up straight. I can't hold you up much
7   longer. *(No answer. PEYTON has a spaced-out look on his face.)*
8   Peyton?
9   TAYLOR: It's no use. He's already gone.
10   JORDAN: Peyton, you've got to stay with us. *(She turns*
11   *PEYTON's head toward her, then lets it flop facing Center Stage.*
12   *PEYTON continues to look spaced out.)*
13   TAYLOR: Face it, we're doomed. We're never going to make it.
14   *(SARAH enters. She walks casually at first, then sees the three at*
15   *Center Stage and runs toward them.)*
16   SARAH: Taylor, Jordan, Peyton, what's the matter?
17   JORDAN: Stay back, Sarah. You might get hurt.
18   SARAH: Are you sick?
19   JORDAN: We're ... we're *Lenten-ized!*
20   SARAH: You're what?
21   TAYLOR: We took a vow to abstain during Lent.
22   SARAH: So?
23   JORDAN: We just can't do it. The pressure is too great.
24   SARAH: What did you give up?
25   JORDAN and TAYLOR: *(Together)* Jelly bread!
26   SARAH: You're kidding, right?
27   JORDAN: It's not just *any* jelly bread, it's Super-Duper
28   Smacker Seedless Boysenberry.
29   PEYTON: *(Longingly echoing JORDAN)* Boysenber-ryyyy.
30   JORDAN: Peyton is starting to come around. Can you hear us,
31   Peyton?
32   PEYTON: *(In a trance)* Jel-lyyyy.
33   SARAH: Wow. This is serious! How long have you given up
34   jelly bread?
35   TAYLOR: *(Looks at watch.)* About ... twenty minutes.
36   SARAH: Twenty minutes? You're never going to make it forty

1   days at this rate.

2   TAYLOR: Forty days?!

3   SARAH: Sure. After "Fat Tuesday" comes forty days before

4   Jesus' resurrection. Those are the days of Lent.

5   TAYLOR: *(To JORDAN)* You said it was forty minutes.

6   SARAH: Forty minutes?

7   TAYLOR: I thought we were halfway through.

8   JORDAN: Why would anybody give *anything* up for forty

9   days?

10   SARAH: I guess so we can remember what Jesus did for us. My

11   mom used to give up television and read her Bible during

12   those forty days. She said it was her time to focus on the

13   Lord instead of earthly things.

14   TAYLOR: Wow. And that was in the really old days before blu-

15   rays.

16   PEYTON: Jel-lyyyy.

17   TAYLOR: But what about poor Peyton? He'll never make it.

18   SARAH: Well, if you really, really want to do the Lenten thing,

19   you don't *have* to give up Super-Duper Smacker Seedless

20   Boysenberry.

21   PEYTON: *(Head pops up. He is suddenly alert and coherent.)* We

22   don't?

23   SARAH: Of course not. Some people give up stuff for Lent, but

24   others use this season to get closer to God and spend time

25   with him.

26   JORDAN: I've got an idea! We can have a Bible study every

27   afternoon.

28   TAYLOR: And we can talk about all the wonderful things Jesus

29   has done for us.

30   PEYTON: And eat jelly bread! Last one to the boysenberry is a

31   Lenten loser! *(PEYTON runs Off-stage, followed by TAYLOR*

32   *and JORDAN.)*

33   SARAH: *(To audience)* How silly — all this fuss over jelly. *(Calls*

34   *Off-stage.)* Hey, save some for me, will ya? *(SARAH exits.)*

Grains of Sand

Theme
God's love, creation of the universe

Scripture Reference
Psalm 8:3, 33:6, 136:7; Matthew 6:26; John 3:16

Synopsis
An explanation of the universe can be overwhelming until the "Jesus factor" is added.

Cast
Bull
Scientist

Costumes
A lab jacket for the scientist

Props
A telescope

Setting
Outside, looking at the night sky

1   (*SCIENTIST stands at Center Stage, looking through telescope.*)
2   SCIENTIST: This is incredible! Hey Bull, come look at all the
3   stars.
4   BULL: (*Enters and looks through telescope.*) **Pretty lights.**
5   SCIENTIST: Did you know that each one represents a sun just
6   like ours?
7   BULL: There must be millions of them!
8   SCIENTIST: And look, do you see what looks like a star just off
9   of Orion's belt?
10   BULL: Yeah.
11   SCIENTIST: That's Andromeda, the nearest galaxy to ours.
12   BULL: No way!
13   SCIENTIST: Amazing, isn't it?
14   BULL: Yeah, but … What's a galaxy?
15   SCIENTIST: It's a place like our galaxy that has billions of
16   stars.
17   BULL: Are you saying there are billions of stars coming from
18   that tiny little speck?
19   SCIENTIST: Exactly.
20   BULL: Wow, the people must be teeny tiny.
21   SCIENTIST: How do you figure?
22   BULL: It's obvious, isn't it? That little speck is no bigger than a
23   grain of sand.
24   SCIENTIST: They may be a grain of sand from where we're
25   standing, Bull, but did you know that some of those stars
26   are three times the size of our own sun?
27   BULL: No kidding?
28   SCIENTIST: It's just that they're so far away that they appear
29   little.
30   BULL: Oh, I get it. It's kind of like a bird in the sky. It looks
31   little when it's up in the air, but it gets bigger when it
32   lands on your lawn — that is, until the cat gets to it.
33   SCIENTIST: And beyond Andromeda are hundreds of
34   thousands more galaxies, each containing a billions stars
35   as well.
36   BULL: Whoa! The universe must be huge!

1   SCIENTIST: It is an infinite expanse of space and time. Some
2   even say there are more stars out in space than grains of
3   sand.
4   BULL: Wow. This is, like, too much information for a guy like
5   me. I mean, it makes me feel sort of —
6   SCIENTIST: Insignificant?
7   BULL: I was aiming for "small," but I'll go with your fancy
8   wording. It's, just, what does this mean for me? It's like
9   my life is nothing compared to the whole expanse of
10   space.
11 SCIENTIST: Ah, but consider this: there may be more stars in
12   the universe than sand on the beach, yet the Lord cares
13   about *you.*
14 BULL: Me?
15 SCIENTIST: Absolutely.
16 BULL: Then God considers me important!
17 SCIENTIST: So important, as a matter of fact, that he sent his
18   Son to die on a cross so you can go to heaven.
19 BULL: Wow. You sure do know a lot of things.
20 SCIENTIST: It's the scientist in me. I see things where there is
21   infinite vastness and infinite smallness, and I can't help
22   but speculate on the deeper meaning of it all.
23 BULL: Yeah. *(Pauses to think for a second.)* What if c-a-t really
24   spelled bird?
25 SCIENTIST: *(Raises eyebrows in surprise.)* Whoa, that's deep,
26   Bull. I didn't think you had it in you.
27 BULL: It comes and goes. *(BOTH exit.)*

The Greatest Risk on Earth

Theme
Love

Scripture Reference
John 3:14-16, 15:12-13, 1 Corinthians 1:17-18, 12:1-11

Synopsis
People gather to view a sight so horrifying that they can't understand the implications of such an act, except for one boy who understands what the risk means.

Cast
Ringleader
Liz
Rodney
Florence
Elmer
Joshua

Costumes
Circus costume for Ringmaster, with top hat, cane, and cloak

Props
None

Setting
The circus. Place a curtain or piece of cardboard hiding either a large crucifix or an actor portraying Jesus on the cross at Center Stage.

1 (*RINGMASTER stands at Center Stage, soliciting business.*)
2 RINGMASTER: Step right up, ladies and gentlemen, and
3 witness the greatest risk on earth! (*ALL enter.*) Don't be
4 afraid, now. Not everyone can handle what lies behind
5 these curtains.
6 LIZ: (*Raises hand.*) I'd like to see.
7 RINGMASTER: And what a brave lady you are! Careful, now
8 — I wouldn't enter too quickly. (*LIZ enters the curtains,*
9 *screams, and runs out.*)
10 RINGMASTER: That's right, ladies and gentlemen — what lies
11 behind this curtain is not for the faint of heart. It takes a
12 certain type of bravery to accept what your eyes are
13 seeing.
14 RODNEY: I'm willing to give it a try.
15 RINGMASTER: Try? Did I hear try? Perhaps you'd better
16 move along, sonny boy. If you're only going to *try* to see
17 this event, I guarantee you won't be able to handle it.
18 RODNEY: (*Indignant*) Says you. (*Looks inside.*) I can't stand it! It's
19 too weird. (*RODNEY runs to nearest exit.*)
20 FLORENCE: Oh Ringmaster, my husband will look. He's done all
21 kinds of gross things in his life. Nothing frightens him.
22 RINGMASTER: What's your name, sir?
23 ELMER: Elmer.
24 RINGMASTER: And where do you work, Elmer?
25 ELMER: I work for the governor.
26 RINGMASTER: She's right — you *do* have a scary profession.
27 But I'm willing to bet you've never seen anything as risky
28 as what's behind this curtain. (*ELMER takes a peek, then*
29 *turns to RINGMASTER, unemotional.*)
30 ELMER: You're right. That is disturbing.
31 RINGMASTER: Don't you feel like you want to run from it?
32 ELMER: No. I find it full of nonsense, actually.
33 RINGMASTER: Would you like me to explain it to you?
34 ELMER: Wouldn't be the least bit interested. But thank you all
35 the same.
36 FLORENCE: Elmer, what did you see? (*Goes to look behind the*

1   *curtain.)*

2   ELMER: Don't do it, Florence. You're not as strong as I am.

3   FLORENCE: Don't be silly. I've raised seven children! I can

4   handle what lies behind — *(Looks inside.)* Oh my, oh my, oh

5   my. Elmer, let's get out of here. *(FLORENCE runs off with*

6   *ELMER shrugging his shoulders and casually exiting Off-stage*

7   *behind her.)*

8   JOSHUA: I'd like to see, mister.

9   RINGMASTER: Beat it, kid. I don't want to give you

10   nightmares.

11   JOSHUA: But I'm brave! I even ate a whole mouthful of

12   jalapeños on a dare.

13   RINGMASTER: What was that like?

14   JOSHUA: I couldn't taste food for a week!

15   RINGMASTER: Hmmmm. Maybe you *are* brave enough. OK,

16   take a look.

17   JOSHUA: *(Looks inside.)* That's not scary at all.

18   RINGMASTER: Are you kidding me? It's intimidating to the

19   rest of the people. Why aren't you frightened?

20   JOSHUA: *(Opens curtain and reveals Christ on the cross.)* Because

21   it's Jesus.

22   RINGMASTER: It's a man hanging on a stick! Look, you can see

23   the blood running down his arms. And look, you can tell he's

24   been beaten to a pulp before he was even hung there.

25   JOSHUA: But he chose to suffer for me. And he chose to suffer

26   for you, too.

27   RINGMASTER: It frightens people to see this.

28   JOSHUA: They shouldn't be frightened.

29   RINGMASTER: It's all nonsense, kid. Why would a man be

30   willing to die such a horrible death?

31   JOSHUA: Because he loved us. Jesus said that there is no

32   greater love than someone who lays his life down for his

33   friends *(John 15:13, author's paraphrase).* Jesus gave his life

34   for everyone.

35   RINGMASTER: That's right, kid. Love, especially God's love,

36   is the greatest risk on earth.

How Healthy Are Your Five Parts?
Part 1

Theme
Worship

Scripture Reference
Psalm 22:2, 149:1; 1 Peter 2:9

Synopsis
An angel teacher tries to teach a bunch of dense
student angels the value of worship.

Cast
Angel
Christian (Female)
Student 1
Student 2
Student 3

Note: This sketch can be downsized to three people by interacting
with one student, or increased to a cast of nine.

Costumes
Angel attire, "wild" clothing for Christian (stripes mixed
with plaid, clashing colors, etc.) with bad hair and
excessive makeup

Props
Pointer stick and iPod.

Setting
Classroom with whiteboard and Christian's home.
The whiteboard has a drawing of a stick figure with a line
coming from the figure's heart.

The lyrics of "Majesty" are used by permission of Jack Hayford Ministries.

1   (*ANGEL is at whiteboard. STUDENTS 1-3 sit by whiteboard.*
2   *CHRISTIAN freezes in place on the other side of the stage.*)
3   **ANGEL: Good evening, fellow angels, and welcome to**
4   **Christian Walk 101.** Today we will be discussing the five
5   basic parts of the Christian walk. Observe the Christian.
6   (*Goes over to CHRISTIAN, who is frozen in time, and points at*
7   *her with her stick.*) **Note the iPod headphones and the total**
8   **oblivion to the world around her. Now watch as we**
9   **release her from the time continuum.** (*She waves her stick at*
10 *her.*)
11 **CHRISTIAN:** (*Starts rapping*)
12   **Oh, I hate my sistah, I hate my brotha,**
13   **And I really hate all of mankind.**
14   **I hate my folks, it ain't no joke**
15   **To drive them outta their mind.**
16 **ANGEL:** (*Waves her stick again. CHRISTIAN freezes.*) **Aside from**
17   **the obvious lack of proper grammar, what did we learn**
18   **here?**
19 **STUDENT 1:** (*Raises her hand and stands up.*) **Oh, I know — she**
20   **has no style when it comes to clothing.**
21 **ANGEL: True, stripes and plaids have never been in vogue,**
22   **which makes this particular person a rebel to her society**
23   **or fashionably clueless. What else?**
24 **STUDENT 2: She's got too much makeup on, and her hair is**
25   **horrible.**
26 **ANGEL: OK, let's get past the outward appearance and focus**
27   **on the inside. What have you noticed is her biggest flaw?**
28 **STUDENT 3: She sings off-key?**
29 **ANGEL:** (*Looks up.*) **Give me patience, Lord.** (*To STUDENTS*)
30   **The words! What is she saying in the words?**
31 **STUDENT: Well, she seems displeased with her family life.**
32 **STUDENT 2: Yeah, she has a few issues.**
33 **STUDENT 3: Do you think her music has anything to do with**
34   **it?**
35 **ANGEL: Praise the Lord, you got it! Angry music creates anger**
36   **in the heart. What this Christian lacks in her life is**

1   worship! Worship is an expression of love to the Lord for
2   all he has provided. It is the basic nutrient in a Christian's
3   walk. Watch what happens when we change the music on
4   her. *(ANGEL waves her stick toward the CHRISTIAN.)*
5   CHRISTIAN: Oh, I hate my — *(Stops and listens.)*
6   OFF-STAGE MUSIC: *(Last line of "Majesty")* Majesty, worship
7   his majesty, Jesus who died, now glorified, King of all
8   kings.
9   CHRISTIAN: *(Looks Off-stage.)* Hey mom, let me help you bring
10   in the groceries! *(Exits.)*
11   ANGEL: You see how worship is the number-one emphasis in
12   creating a healthy five-part Christian?
13   STUDENT 1: So they'll bring in the groceries?
14   ANGEL: How in the world did you get into heaven when
15   you're so clueless?
16   STUDENT 1: I don't know. By sheer grace, I suppose.
17   ANGEL: *(Softening)* As we all did. Class dismissed. *(Goes to*
18   *whiteboard and draws a line from the stick figure's heart and*
19   *writes the word "Worship" at the end of the line as STUDENTS*
20   *file out.)*

How Healthy Are Your Five Parts?
Part 2

Theme
Fellowship, loving others

Scripture Reference
Psalm 55:14, Hebrews 3:13

Synopsis
Angel teaches her class about fellowship
and the choices Christians make.

Cast
Angel
Student 1
Student 2
Student 3
Christian
Julie
Maggie

Costumes
Angel attire

Props
A pointer stick

Setting
Classroom with whiteboard and at school. The whiteboard
has a stick figure with a line drawn from the heart
area that says "worship."

1   (*ANGEL is at whiteboard. STUDENTS 1-3 sit by whiteboard.*
2   *CHRISTIAN and two friends, JULIE and MAGGIE, are frozen*
3   *in time on the other side of the stage.*)
4   **ANGEL: Good morning, class. Welcome to Christian Walk 101.**
5   **Today we will discuss part two of the Christian**
6   **experience: fellowship. Observe the Christian. Notice she**
7   **is approached by two people.** (*ANGEL waves her pointy*
8   *stick.*)
9   **JULIE: So are you coming with us or not? It's supposed to be a**
10   **wild party.**
11   **MAGGIE: But you promised to attend the youth rally with me,**
12   **remember?**
13   **JULIE: Youth rally? How boring can that be? Our party puts**
14   **any rally to shame.**
15   **MAGGIE: I don't doubt that.**
16   **JULIE: What do you mean by that?**
17   **MAGGIE: Nothing, except everyone knows your parties are**
18   **morally questionable.**
19   **JULIE: You got a problem with that?**
20   **MAGGIE: As a matter of fact, I do.**
21   **JULIE:** (*To CHRISTIAN*) **Come on, let's blow this joint.**
22   **CHRISTIAN: Well … uh, I did promise to go with Maggie to**
23   **the rally.**
24   **JULIE: Are you kidding? You don't want to be labeled as one of**
25   **them! No one will speak to you at school. Do you really**
26   **want that?**
27   **ANGEL:** (*Waves her stick and ALL freeze.*) **Now class, what are we**
28   **learning from this conversation?**
29   **STUDENT 1:** (*Raises hand and stands.*) **That Julie puts on really**
30   **cool parties!**
31   **ANGEL: That's not the answer I was looking for. Notice our**
32   **Christian has to make a choice between fellowship with**
33   **worldly people, or fellowship with Christians like her.**
34   **STUDENT 2: I sure do feel sorry for our Christian.**
35   **STUDENT 3: So do I. She doesn't stand a chance.**
36   **ANGEL: Don't you think she'll have just as much fun singing**

1   and learning about the Word of God with other Christians
2   who are like her?
3   STUDENT 1: Sure, but to choose openly in front of the most
4   popular girl in school is social suicide!
5   STUDENT 2: I couldn't have done it.
6   STUDENT 1: It's a good thing you're already in heaven.
7   STUDENT 2: I know! I dodged a bullet on that one, wouldn't
8   you say?
9   ANGEL: Let's take a look and see the choice our Christian
10   makes, shall we?
11   STUDENT 1: It's your pointy stick. *(ANGEL waves her stick.)*
12   CHRISTIAN: Julie, I'm sorry, but I really don't want to go to
13   your party.
14   JULIE: Are you kidding me? I can't believe you're ditching me!
15   CHRISTIAN: I'm doing no such thing. I've been looking
16   forward to this rally, and I really want to go. We can hang
17   out some other time.
18   JULIE: I seriously doubt it. *(Turns and exits.)*
19   ANGEL: Our Christian has made excellent strides in her walk
20   with Christ by choosing fellowship with other believers.
21   Psalm 55:14 talks about Christians taking "sweet counsel
22   together" *(Author's paraphrase)*. Isn't that wonderful?
23   STUDENT 1: I'm late for my harp lesson. *(She exits.)*
24   STUDENT 2: I've got choir practice. *(Exits.)*
25   ANGEL: *(To STUDENT 3)* Did you at least get the message from
26   the lesson?
27   STUDENT 3: I sure did.
28   ANGEL: Really? And what did you learn?
29   STUDENT 3: It's more fun to sing with the saints than rap with
30   the rebels.
31   ANGEL: You get an "A." Class dismissed. *(All STUDENTS exit.*
32   *ANGEL draws a line from the stick figure's head and writes*
33   *"fellowship.")*

How Healthy Are Your Five Parts?
Part 3

Theme
Discipleship

Scripture Reference
Matthew 10:32; Luke 21:14-18

Synopsis
Christian learns that taking a stand sometimes means standing alone.

Cast
Angel
Student 1
Student 2
Christian
Danielle
Erica
Bonnie
Sinful Nature

Costumes
Angel attire and a shirt with "Sinful Nature" written on the front.

Props
Pointer stick

Setting
Classroom with whiteboard and at school. The whiteboard has a stick figure in the middle with a line coming from the heart that says "worship." Another line extends from the head saying "fellowship."

1   (*ANGEL is at whiteboard. STUDENTS 1-3 sit by whiteboard.*
2   *CHRISTIAN freezes in place.*)
3   ANGEL: Welcome, students, to Christian Walk 101. Today we
4   discuss the importance of discipleship. Anyone know
5   what discipleship means? (*STUDENT 1 raises hand.*)
6   STUDENT 1: Is it the ship the disciples sailed on with Jesus?
7   ANGEL: Close, my little clueless wonder, but not good enough.
8   Discipleship is learning to stand before others and declare
9   your belief in God.
10   STUDENT 2: Well, duh. We do that all the time here.
11   ANGEL: True, we have no problem confessing that Jesus is Lord
12   in our own secure realm. But Christian down there — she's
13   having a terrible time. (*Points to CHRISTIAN on the other side of*
14   *the stage, frozen in time.*) Notice what happens when some
15   friends of hers challenge her. (*ANGEL waves her stick. Three*
16   *friends enter, BONNIE, DANIELLE, and ERICA.*)
17   BONNIE: There she is.
18   DANIELLE: Christian, you've got to solve a question for us.
19   CHRISTIAN: Sure. What's your question?
20   ERICA: Is it true you're a follower of Jesus?
21   CHRISTIAN: What? (*SINFUL NATURE runs up behind her.*)
22   SINFUL NATURE: Quick, quick, answer with a question,
23   answer with a question.
24   CHRISTIAN: Why would you ask such a thing?
25   DANIELLE: Well, Rosie told Sally who told Rebecca who told
26   me that you went to some church meeting the night of
27   Brian's big party.
28   SINFUL NATURE: Quick, make an accusation. Change the
29   subject.
30   CHRISTIAN: I thought Rosie went to jail.
31   ERICA: Her dad bailed her out. Answer the question.
32   SINFUL NATURE: Divert, divert. Throw snob girl a little
33   attitude.
34   CHRISTIAN: Who are you, and what do you care about my
35   life?
36   ERICA: (*Rolls her eyes and lets out a loud sigh.*) I told you she

1   wouldn't admit it.
2   CHRISTIAN: *(Points at ERICA.)* Who is this creature?
3   BONNIE: Erica is our new friend.
4   CHRISTIAN: What am I, chopped liver?
5   DANIELLE: It depends.
6   CHRISTIAN: Depends on what?
7   SINFUL NATURE: Warning, warning, dangerous territory
8   here. Look for quick exit or escape route.
9   DANIELLE: It depends on how you answer the question.
10   SINFUL NATURE: Stall time. Big, big stall.
11   CHRISTIAN: What is the question again?
12   ERICA: Are you a Christian or not? *(ANGEL waves her stick and
13   all freeze.)*
14   ANGEL: Our Christian is facing the toughest challenge of her
15   life. It hasn't been long since she became a Christian, but
16   can she stand the pressure of her peers?
17   STUDENT 1: *(Stands.)* Twenty halos says she cracks under
18   pressure.
19   STUDENT 2: *(Stands.)* I bet thirty halos.
20   STUDENT 1: I bet thirty halos and a harp.
21   ANGEL: Sit down! *(Both STUDENTS drop to the floor.)* This is not
22   a gambling station, although I admit if I were a betting
23   angel, I would not hold out much hope for our little
24   Christian. Look at her, so pathetic. She's trying to listen to
25   her own misguided advice, but it's just leading her deeper
26   into a hole. Eventually she will have to make a decision
27   about her relationship with Christ, and you know what
28   that means?
29   STUDENT 1: Yeah. Good-bye, social life.
30   STUDENT 2: She'll be ostracized from the in crowd.
31   ANGEL: Let's find out, shall we? *(She waves her stick and the
32   attention goes back to CHRISTIAN and her FRIENDS.)*
33   CHRISTIAN: What was the question again?
34   ERICA: Are you a Christian or not?
35   SINFUL NATURE: Don't do this. Whatever you do, don't admit
36   it.

1   CHRISTIAN: Yes. I am a believer and follower of Jesus. *(ALL*
2   *groan.)*
3   BONNIE: I can't believe you said that.
4   ERICA: I told you she was one of them.
5   BONNIE: And to think you were once my best friend.
6   CHRISTIAN: I'm still your friend.
7   BONNIE: Sorry, Christian, but I have a reputation to uphold. I
8   can't be seen with you. *(Half wave)* **Later.** *(BONNIE and*
9   *ERICA exit.)*
10   DANIELLE: I can't believe you actually admitted it, Christian.
11   CHRISTIAN: Yeah, well, you probably think I'm a freak now.
12   DANIELLE: No, I don't.
13   CHRISTIAN: You don't?
14   DANIELLE: No. I'm a Christian too, but I've never had the guts
15   to admit it.
16   CHRISTIAN: I almost didn't. Everything in me was fighting to
17   deny it. *(SINFUL NATURE slinks away.)* **But I love Jesus,**
18   **and if being a believer means a few less friends, then I'm**
19   **better without them.**
20   DANIELLE: You're really brave, Christian. Can I go with you to
21   your next meeting?
22   CHRISTIAN: You bet.
23   DANIELLE: Just don't tell anybody. *(DANIELLE and*
24   *CHRISTIAN exit.)*
25   ANGEL: Now, what have we learned, my sorry little cherubs?
26   STUDENT 2: *(Raises hand.)* **Never place a bet on a teenager?**
27   ANGEL: *(Sighs.)* **I've got to get a new class.** *(STUDENTS exit.*
28   *ANGEL goes over to the whiteboard, draws a line from the stick*
29   *figure's mouth, writes "discipleship," then exits.)*

How Healthy Are Your Five Parts?
Part 4

Theme
Ministry, loving people in need

Scripture Reference
Matthew 10:32, Luke 21:14-18

Synopsis
Christian learns the art of giving.

Cast
Angel
Student 1
Student 2
Student 3
Christian
Darrin
Mrs. Jones

Costumes
Angel and Students wear white robes or choir robes and
Christian is dressed in stripes and plaids.

Props
Pointer stick and two bags of groceries

Setting
Classroom with whiteboard and outside a poor woman's
home. The whiteboard has a stick figure in the middle with a
line coming from the heart that says "Worship." Another line
extends from the head saying "fellowship," and a third line
comes out of the mouth and says "discipline."

1   (*ANGEL is at whiteboard. STUDENTS 1-3 sit by whiteboard.*
2   *CHRISTIAN freezes in place.*)
3   ANGEL: All righty, class, today we will learn about the subject
4   of ministry. Does anyone know what ministry is all
5   about?
6   STUDENT 1: (*Raises hand and stands.*) Oh, I know. It's Jesus!
7   ANGEL: Give that angel a star for the day.
8   STUDENT 2: Showoff.
9   ANGEL: And what does ministry do?
10   STUDENT 1: Oh, I know. We show God's love by our actions
11   toward others.
12   ANGEL: Excellent! My, someone did their homework, didn't
13   they?
14   STUDENT 3: (*To STUDENT 1*) Hey, sit down before you make
15   us all look bad.
16   STUDENT 2: Yeah, no one likes a holier-than-thou angel.
17   ANGEL: As we study our Christian, we learn that ministry is in
18   the hands of the believer because the hands serve others.
19   (*Draws a line from the stick figure's hands and writes the word*
20   *"ministry."*) Let's watch our little Christian as she and a
21   fellow believer practice the art of giving to those in need.
22   (*She waves her stick. CHRISTIAN and DARRIN enter carrying*
23   *bags of groceries.*)
24   DARRIN: So why did we buy all these things, Christian?
25   CHRISTIAN: We're helping this poor woman in need. Her
26   husband died, so we're following Scripture by providing
27   for her and her children.
28   DARRIN: Where does it say that?
29   CHRISTIAN: James 1:27 says to look after orphans and widows
30   in their suffering.
31   DARRIN: What do you think will happen when we show up
32   with these things?
33   CHRISTIAN: Well, first I think she'll be pleasantly surprised.
34   Then she'll be embarrassed, because she knows that *we*
35   know that she's having a rough time of it. Then she'll
36   probably try to tell us she's not as bad off as we think she

1   is, however, she'll be grateful that we brought the items
2   and she'll take them from us "just because we went to the
3   trouble" to get them, but secretly she'll be relieved that
4   she doesn't have to worry about food for the next several
5   weeks. She'll still be concerned about how she's going to
6   come up with the money when the food's all gone,
7   however, she'll be thankful for the food she has for today.
8   DARRIN: How can you think of all those things without
9   getting a headache?
10   CHRISTIAN: Trust me, it's in a woman's nature.
11   DARRIN: You mean you can't just sit on a couch and not think
12   of anything at all?
13   CHRISTIAN: Who can do that?
14   DARRIN: Most guys.
15   CHRISTIAN: Really? That's weird. *(MRS. JONES enters.)* Hello,
16   Mrs. Jones.
17   MRS. JONES: Christian, Darrin, what a pleasant surprise.
18   What brings you to our little neighborhood?
19   CHRISTIAN: We brought you food for the next two weeks.
20   MRS. JONES: Food? For us? Oh, you shouldn't have. We may
21   be a little tight right now, but the Lord is taking good care
22   of us.
23   CHRISTIAN: Oh, we know that, Mrs. Jones. But you know the
24   ministry committee, they're always looking for someone
25   to serve.
26   MRS. JONES: They are an eager lot.
27   CHRISTIAN: Besides, by giving you this food, they really feel
28   like they're doing something special for the Lord. Won't
29   you help us out?
30   MRS. JONES: Well, we don't really need it, but I'll take it just
31   for you.
32   CHRISTIAN: Thank you, Mrs. Jones. You're really helping to
33   develop our group's spirit of giving.
34   MRS. JONES: Anything for you, Christian. *(She takes the*
35   *packages from CHRISTIAN and DARRIN and, as she turns*
36   *away from them, she faces the audience, looks up, and mouths the*

1   *words "thank you," then freezes.)*
2   **DARRIN:** So did all those emotions we talked about just
3   happen?
4   **CHRISTIAN:** You didn't see it?
5   **DARRIN:** *(Raises his arms, palms up in confusion.)* **See what?** *(Exits*
6   *with CHRISTIAN.)*
7   **ANGEL:** So class, what did we learn today?
8   **STUDENT 1:** That you have to lie about giving charitable gifts
9   because the ego of the human is all messed up?
10   **ANGEL:** Wrong, my little dimwitted one. *(To STUDENT 2)*
11   What about you?
12   **STUDENT 2:** Um, what was the question again?
13   **ANGEL:** *(Growing impatient)* What is the answer to today's
14   question?
15   **STUDENT 2:** Uh ... *(Looks around for help. STUDENT 3, seeing*
16   *she's faltering, raises her hand.)* **Jesus?**
17   **STUDENT 3:** No fair. Jesus is always the right answer.
18   **ANGEL:** That's right. Whatever we do, we do it for the Lord and
19   not humans. Because Jesus loves us, we show that love by
20   helping others in need. Class dismissed. *(ALL exit.)*

How Healthy Are Your Five Parts?
Part 5

Theme
Evangelism

Scripture Reference
Matthew 28:19-20; John 4:35-38

Synopsis
Christian faces her first attempt at evangelism

Cast
Angel
Student 1
Student 2
Christian
Old Man

Costumes
Hideous clothing — stripes, plaids, and polka dots for
Christian. Old Man wears a plaid shirt and
mismatched pants hiked up past his belly button.

Props
Bible and pointer stick

Setting
A classroom with a whiteboard and a nursing home. The
whiteboard has a stick figure in the middle with a line coming
from the heart that says "worship." Another line extends from
the head saying "fellowship," and a third line comes out of the
mouth and says "discipline." The fourth line is by the hands and
says "ministry." The last line is drawn from the feet with the
word "evangelism" written off to the side.

1   *(ANGEL is at whiteboard. STUDENTS 1 and 2 sit by*
2   *whiteboard. CHRISTIAN freezes in place.)*
3   ANGEL: Welcome again, students, to the final session of
4   Christian Walk 101. Today you can see our little Christian
5   exploring unknown territory. *(Points to CHRISTIAN*
6   *clutching her Bible, frozen in time.)*
7   STUDENT 1: She looks scared.
8   STUDENT 2: Can you blame her? Look how she's dressed!
9   ANGEL: Now, now — the type of clothes one wears does not
10   diminish from the message of the Word.
11   STUDENT 2: Maybe not, but it sure distracts. Polka dots and
12   plaids? You'd think becoming a Christian would have
13   given her a little bit of taste.
14   ANGEL: Becoming a Christian means she's forgiven, not
15   perfect. However, let's focus on the task at hand. *(Points*
16   *toward CHRISTIAN.)* Notice our little Christian at a
17   nursing home, getting ready to tell these wonderful
18   people about Jesus because why, class?
19   STUDENTS 1 and 2: *(In unison)* Because if you're not talking
20   about Jesus, you're off the subject.
21   ANGEL: Exactly. Let's see how our little Christian does. *(Waves*
22   *her stick and CHRISTIAN begins to wander Downstage.)*
23   CHRISTIAN: Wow. It's really scary here. It kind of smells, too.
24   *(Sighs.)* Be brave, Christian. You can do it. *(An OLD MAN*
25   *enters.)*
26   OLD MAN: Hello there, little lady.
27   CHRISTIAN: Uh, hi.
28   OLD MAN: Hey, nice shirt you got there.
29   CHRISTIAN: Thanks.
30   STUDENT 1: Oh, I can't watch. She's going to blow it for sure.
31   OLD MAN: What brings you to our neck of the woods?
32   CHRISTIAN: We're here to tell everyone about Jesus.
33   OLD MAN: Jesus, huh? Never had much use for him myself.
34   CHRISTIAN: Can I ask you something? If you were to die
35   today, do you believe you'd go to heaven?
36   OLD MAN: I think so. I've tried to be good all my life.

1 CHRISTIAN: Did you know that the Scriptures say that
2   nobody is worthy enough to get into heaven? It doesn't
3   matter how good you think you might be. It's never
4   enough.
5 OLD MAN: So tell me, if the things I did in my life don't credit
6   me anything, how does a fellow like me get to heaven?
7 CHRISTIAN: All you have to do is believe in Jesus. That's why
8   he came. That's why he died on the cross for you.
9 OLD MAN: Tell me more. *(They exit.)*
10 ANGEL: This is a big moment in our Christian's life. Next
11   week that gentleman is going to be called home, and his
12   name will be written in the Book of Life.
13 STUDENT 1: Then Christian did it! She actually led someone
14   on the right path!
15 STUDENT 2: Wow, I didn't think she had it in her.
16 ANGEL: After watching Christian grow, you still doubted her
17   abilities?
18 STUDENT 2: Well, yeah. It's not like there's anything special
19   about her.
20 STUDENT 1: I know. She's just sort of ...
21 STUDENT 2: Ordinary.
22 STUDENT 1: Yes.
23 ANGEL: The Word is not about flash and fancy. It's ordinary
24   people sharing their knowledge and experience about
25   Christ because ...
26 ALL: *(Together)* If you're not talking about Jesus, you're off the
27   subject!
28 ANGEL: Class dismissed. *(ALL exit.)*

Hypocritically Speaking

Theme
Hypocrisy, Lent

Scripture Reference
Matthew 6:5; Matthew 23:27; John 8:1-11

Synopsis
A Pharisee and Sadducee discuss "spiritual issues."

Cast
Pharisee
Sadducee
Martha
Sarah
Extra

Costumes
Biblical robes

Props
None

Setting
Jerusalem in Jesus' time.

1   *(A PHARISEE stands at Center Stage, arms raised in prayer.*
2   *SADDUCEE stands next to him.)*
3   PHARISEE: O holy Father, protect these fine citizens. Forgive
4   them of their many, many, *many* sins.
5   SADDUCEE: *(Looks around.)* You're wasting your breath. No
6   one's around!
7   PHARISEE: Where is everyone?
8   SADDUCEE: They're all listening to that Nazarene guy outside
9   of town.
10   PHARISEE: The nerve of him. I even got up early so everyone
11   would see me praying in the streets.
12   SADDUCEE: And you even put on your best robes.
13   PHARISEE: I know! How dare he steal my thunder!
14   SADDUCEE: Quick — here comes some people.
15   PHARISEE: *(Quickly raises his arms and speaks loudly.)* Bless this
16   day. Make your grace shine around them, wash them with
17   your goodness ...
18   SARAH: *(Walking in quickly, stopping only to speak)* Come on,
19   Martha. Jesus is this way.
20   MARTHA: *(Enters and walks across stage while speaking.)* Oh, I
21   hope we haven't missed him! *(BOTH exit.)*
22   SADDUCEE: They're gone.
23   PHARISEE: May thunderclouds rain on Jesus and his
24   followers.
25   SADDUCEE: There's got to be some way to expose this Jesus
26   for the hypocrite he is.
27   PHARISEE: How dare he call himself a teacher! He doesn't
28   even show the basic understanding of what it takes to
29   lead these people.
30   SADDUCEE: *(Disgusted)* Showing compassion to sinners.
31   PHARISEE: *(Shakes head.)* Healing on the Sabbath.
32   SADDUCEE: Not just any healing. Lepers, of all people!
33   PHARISEE: You'd think he would know not to heal anyone so
34   diseased!
35   SADDUCEE: Leprosy is God's judgment. Lepers should just
36   accept their plight and live in isolation with the rest of the

1   worms of the earth.

2   PHARISEE: As far as I'm concerned, most of the people are —

3   *(EXTRA enters, walking across stage. PHARISEE quickly raises*

4   *his arms)* God's holy people, the chosen ones from the God

5   of Abraham, Isaac, and Esau —

6   SADDUCEE: Jacob.

7   PHARISEE: *(Quickly)* Jacob. Bless them, O bless them most,

8   holy Father. *(When the EXTRA has exited, he drops his arms.)*

9   You'd think they would at least acknowledge the effort

10   I'm putting in here.

11   SADDUCEE: It's all Jesus' fault. He's turning the crowd against

12   us, I tell you. I even heard him imply that we were not

13   sincere in our teachings and practices.

14   PHARISEE: *(Shocked expression)* That's ... that's heresy! You're

15   telling me he's saying we're not spiritual?

16   SADDUCEE: I even heard him suggest that *we* are sinners.

17   PHARISEE: That's it! The man has to go.

18   SADDUCEE: The sooner the better.

19   PHARISEE: I've got an idea. Let's pay a little visit to that

20   woman of the evening that lives up the way.

21   SADDUCEE: That's a great idea! There's no one around to catch

22   us.

23   PHARISEE: Not for you, you idiot. We're going to use her to

24   trap Jesus with his own words.

25   SADDUCEE: How?

26   PHARISEE: We're going to throw her at his feet, and then ask

27   him what the law says about her kind.

28   SADDUCEE: And because he loves sinners so much, he'll try to

29   save her from stoning.

30   PHARISEE: The moment he does that, he becomes guilty of the

31   law himself, and we'll be able to stone him along with

32   her.

33   SADDUCEE: It seems an awful waste of a good prostitute,

34   though.

35   PHARISEE: Sacrifices sometimes must be made for the general

36   good.

I Got the Memo

Theme
Prayer, prayer warriors.

Scripture Reference
Matthew 2:22; 1 John 5:4

Synopsis
A clerical angel learns what can happen when
a prayer warrior is on the attack.

Cast
Angel
Messenger 1
Messenger 2
Messenger 3
Note: You may combine the Messenger
parts for smaller groups.

Costumes
Angel costumes or choir robes work well.

Props
Lots of paper. One trick is to cover books with papers
for the appearance of bulk. You will also need an
inkpad and stamp and a trash bag.

Setting
Heaven. You will need a table with boxes marked
"Incoming," "Outgoing," and "Cathy's Box."

Note: This is a great last-minute sketch, as all the lines may be
written on the pages that are handed back and forth.

1   *(The scene begins with ANGEL sitting at a table with two piles of*
2   *papers, one labeled "incoming," the other labeled "outgoing." He*
3   *stamps a piece of paper and places it in the outgoing box.*
4   *MESSENGER 1 enters.)*
5   **MESSENGER 1: Got a prayer request for you. It's from Cathy.**
6   **ANGEL: Put it in my incoming box.** *(Hands him the paper from the*
7   *outgoing box.)* **Here, this prayer is from Tom Billingsworth.**
8   **It's been approved. Make sure it's filled to order.**
9   **MESSENGER 1: It shall be done.** *(MESSENGER 1 exits.*
10   *MESSENGER 2 enters.)*
11   **MESSENGER 2: Got another prayer from Cathy. Where do you**
12   **want it?**
13   **ANGEL: Put it in my incoming box. Here,** *(Stamps a paper and*
14   *hands it to MESSENGER 2)* **take these two to the "do not**
15   **answer" pile.**
16   **MESSENGER 2:** *(Looking at the papers)* **More prayers for the**
17   **winning lottery ticket?**
18   **ANGEL:** *(Shakes his head.)* **We must get over a hundred thousand**
19   **a day. I haven't even gotten to the quick prayers from**
20   **Vegas.** *(MESSENGER 2 exits as MESSENGER 3 enters.)*
21   **MESSENGER 3: Another prayer from Cathy.**
22   **ANGEL: Put it in my pile.** *(Stamps a page and hands it to*
23   *MESSENGER 3.)* **Here, take this one. I've marked it as**
24   **approved, although they're going to have to wait six**
25   **months until we get everything lined up.** *(MESSENGER 3*
26   *takes the paper and exits.)*
27   **MESSENGER 1:** *(Enters.)* **I've got two prayers from Cathy and**
28   **three prayers from Cathy's relatives.**
29   **ANGEL: Let me see those.** *(Examines the pages.)* **Hmmmm — I**
30   **see her son has gone the route of the prodigal. OK, put it**
31   **in my "in" pile and I'll start looking into it.** *(Stamps a page*
32   *and hands it to MESSENGER 1.)* **Here, take this prayer and**
33   **get our team working on it.**
34   **MESSENGER 1:** *(Examines the page.)* **Courtney is looking for a**
35   **friend?**
36   **ANGEL: Cute, huh? She's riding her bike around the block**

1   because she read the passage to "seek and you shall find."
2   She's not going to find a friend today, or even up to high
3   school, but the Lord has some awesome lifelong friends
4   he's working on for her in college and even up to her
5   adult years. *(MESSENGER 1 exits.)*
6   MESSENGER 2: *(Enters.)* I've got three more prayers from
7   Cathy, two from her parents, seven from her friends, and
8   fifteen from her prayer group.
9   ANGEL: Her prayer group? Put them in the pile, and I will get
10   to them when I can. I can only work one miracle at a time,
11   and this isn't the first time her son went "prodigal" on us.
12   Here, take this prayer and mark it as "unaccepted." We
13   don't curse mother-in-laws, no matter how mean they are.
14   *(MESSENGER 2 exits. MESSENGER 3 enters with a ream of*
15   *paper.)*
16   MESSENGER 3: I've got five more prayers from Cathy, thirty-
17   seven from her prayer group, fifty-seven from her mother
18   and mother in-law's prayer groups combined, twenty-
19   seven from cousins, friends, and co-workers, and seven
20   hundred thirty-four from her church. *(He plunks the entire*
21   *ream in the "in" box.)*
22   ANGEL: Stop already. Doesn't she ever quit? Let me see those.
23   *(Flips through some of the pages.)* OK, it looks like prodigal
24   boy needs another life lesson to get him back to looking
25   to Jesus for the source of his life. Send this out to all
26   available Angels to do whatever it takes to win him back.
27   *(Flips through some more pages.)* Looks like he's hanging
28   with the wrong crowd again.
29   MESSENGER 3: Oh, can I have that one? I love exposing
30   wrong relationships.
31   ANGEL: It's yours. Maybe after we get him back to the flock,
32   Cathy will quit sending all these prayers, and I can get
33   some work done. *(MESSENGER 3 happily exits. ANGEL*
34   *looks upward toward heaven.)* Yes, I know you feel it's
35   important to listen to all prayers, but what are we going to
36   do with this woman who won't stop praying? You can see

1 my paperwork is backing up. *(MESSENGER 1 enters.)*
2 MESSENGER 1: It worked! Her prodigal son is back in the fold
3 and fully repentant. I have a prayer of thanksgiving
4 offered by Cathy and all her prayer warriors. *(Hands him*
5 *several sheets of paper.)*
6 ANGEL: What a relief!
7 MESSENGER 1: However, since she's found out this prayer
8 thing works so well, she's joined three more prayer
9 groups. I have five thousand requests for a neighbor's
10 uncle. *(Hands ANGEL a trash bag full of paper.)*
11 ANGEL: *(Groans.)* What am I going to do with this one? *(Thinks*
12 *for a second.)* I've got it. *(Reaches under the table and pulls out*
13 *another box that says "Cathy's Prayers" and places it next to the*
14 *incoming box. MESSENGER 1 exits. MESSENGER 2 enters*
15 *with large volumes of paper.)*
16 MESSENGER 2: More prayers from Cathy. *(Plunks papers in his*
17 *"in" box, then exits. MESSENGER 1 and MESSENGER 3 enter*
18 *carrying even bigger armloads of prayers.)*
19 ANGEL: All right, hold it! What does Cathy want now?
20 MESSENGER 3: *(Reading from a list)* For the son of a cousin to be
21 healed, for five other people to be healed, seven to find
22 the Lord, one friend of a friend of a friend to have
23 successful surgery ...
24 ANGEL: *(Looks up toward heaven.)* You're enjoying this, aren't
25 you? *(Back to MESSENGER 3)* Are there any lottery
26 requests in there?
27 MESSENGER 3: *(Looking at the list)* No lottery requests.
28 ANGEL: Then the Boss says to grant her prayer requests.
29 MESSENGER 1: All of them?
30 ANGEL: All of them. *(Takes all the papers from the pile and plops*
31 *them in MESSENGER 3's arms.)* Just take them and answer
32 them. Don't bother me anymore. Got it?
33 MESSENGER 3: *(Grunts as he hauls away the papers.)* Got it.
34 MESSENGER 2: *(Enters.)* Got some more prayer requests from
35 Cathy.
36 ANGEL: I just answered a bunch. How much this time?

1 MESSENGER 2: A truckload.
2 ANGEL: Oh man, these prayer warriors never give up! You
3 grant them one small prayer request, and they just keep
4 on praying.
5 MESSENGER 2: Shall I bring them in?
6 ANGEL: I've got the memo! Just give her what she wants as
7 long as it's within reason. *(To audience)* Seeing as she won't
8 give up anyway.
9 MESSENGER 2: These prayer warriors sure are persistent.
10 ANGEL: That's right.
11 MESSENGER 2: I heard that even prodigal boy is praying now.
12 *(ANGEL whimpers, lays his head down on the table, and starts to*
13 *cry.)*

I Only Eat Chocolate for the Health Benefits

Theme
Choices, doctrine

Scripture Reference
John 4:14; 1 Corinthians 3:2; Hebrews 5:13-14

Synopsis
A spiritual argument plays out as two vendors try to persuade a woman to choose which "church diet" to follow.

Cast
Vendor 1
Vendor 2
Woman

Costumes
The Vendors may wear aprons if desired.

Props
Pitcher of water, mug, several platters with lids, steak (can be fake), milk, lots of chocolate, gummi bears, bottle of antacid, a mug, and a coffeepot.

Setting
A food market. Two tables are positioned at opposite ends of the stage.

1	*(Scene begins with two VENDORS positioned behind their*
2	*respective tables at opposite ends of the stage. Table one has the*
3	*meat, milk, and a pitcher of water. Table two has three platters*
4	*with lids and a mug. The WOMAN enters and approaches the*
5	*first table.)*
6	**VENDOR 1: Welcome to our table. Would you like to**
7	**participate in what we have to offer?**
8	**WOMAN: What do you have?**
9	**VENDOR 1:** *(Lifts up the items.)* **Milk and meat.**
10	**WOMAN: Is that all?**
11	**VENDOR 1: Is that all? Why, it's all you'll ever need!**
12	**WOMAN: It seems pretty basic to me.**
13	**VENDOR 1: Milk is basic to the baby Christian. It goes down**
14	**smoothly, it's easy to digest, and it provides the basic**
15	**nutritional need to sustain you in your growth ...**
16	**providing, of course, that you are new to the faith.**
17	**WOMAN: I've gone to church all my life.**
18	**VENDOR 1: Excellent! Then you would probably enjoy the**
19	**meat that we have. There's something for everyone to**
20	**really sink their teeth into.**
21	**VENDOR 2: Are you seriously going to fall for that old line?**
22	**WOMAN: Why? Do you have something better?**
23	**VENDOR 2: I have something that will satisfy all your desires.**
24	*(Lifts a lid to tray 1.)* **Chocolate.**
25	**WOMAN: Chocolate!** *(She walks over to table 2.)*
26	**VENDOR 2: Not just** *any* **chocolate, we have one hundred percent**
27	**lactose soy lecithin, artificially-flavored chocolate.**
28	**WOMAN: I don't know what that means, but it sounds yummy.**
29	**VENDOR 2: And it's rich enough to satisfy whatever you want**
30	**to believe.**
31	**VENDOR 1: That's disgusting. There is absolutely no**
32	**nutritional value in what you have to offer. (***WOMAN nods*
33	*her head in resigned agreement and starts to walk back to table 1.)*
34	**VENDOR 2:** *(Lifts the lid to tray 2.)* **Did I mention we have nuts?**
35	**WOMAN:** *(She immediately turns toward table 2.)* **Nuts?**
36	**VENDOR 2: Soaked in honey and fat. It's pure protein.**

1   VENDOR 1: You're sugar-coating your product. You don't offer
2   anything sound and nutritional. You only give them what
3   they think they want, or what's popular at the time.
4   *(WOMAN starts to walk back to table 1.)*
5   VENDOR 2: Speaking of sugar ... we have Sugar Gummies.
6   *(Holds up a bag of gummi bears.)*
7   WOMAN: *(Immediately turns towards table.)* Sugar Gummies! I
8   love those!
9   VENDOR 2: *(Hands her several.)* We have the best around.
10   Besides, why waste time chewing on meat when one
11   Sugar Gummi will glob on to your teeth for hours?
12   WOMAN: *(Turns toward table with a mouth full of gummi bears.)*
13   Heed dot a point, ya know.
14   VENDOR 2: Careful with the gummies. You don't want to hurt
15   yourself.
16   VENDOR 1: You need something to wash that down. We offer
17   the living water of Christ. One drink, and you will never
18   go thirsty.
19   VENDOR 2: Why waste time with boring water when you can
20   enjoy a nice cup of hot cocoa? *(Holds up a mug.)*
21   WOMAN: Is it diet?
22   VENDOR 2: Are you insane?
23   WOMAN: Sorry, I lost myself for a moment. *(Points at another*
24   *platter.)* What's that?
25   VENDOR 2: *(Lifts the third lid.)* Dark chocolate.
26   WOMAN: Oh. I don't like dark chocolate.
27   VENDOR 2: And why should you? At our table, we let you
28   choose what appeals to you most.
29   WOMAN: So if I don't like what you have to offer ...
30   VENDOR 2: You just throw it out! *(Takes the chocolate and tosses it.)*
31   WOMAN: I like this table!
32   VENDOR 1: But he's not offering you anything that will help
33   you grow! Without a good, sustaining base of milk, meat,
34   and water, you'll die of malnutrition.
35   VENDOR 2: I beg to differ. What is the main ingredient in
36   chocolate?

1 WOMAN: Uh ... sugar?
2 VENDOR 2: I mean besides that.
3 WOMAN: Artificial flavors?
4 VENDOR 2: Besides that.
5 WOMAN: Uh ... milk?
6 VENDOR 2: Yes! Yes, milk is in chocolate!
7 WOMAN: Then it's just as good as the other table!
8 VENDOR 2: And if you eat the fruit and nut bar, you get
9   protein and a freeze-dried fig.
10 VENDOR 1: Soaked in sugar, I'm sure.
11 VENDOR 2: Exactly!
12 WOMAN: Where do I sign up?
13 VENDOR 2: Go down the hall until you reach a room full of
14   fat, lethargic people who can't think for themselves.
15 WOMAN: Thank you. Oh, may I have another Sugar Gummi?
16 VENDOR 2: Take as many as you want. *(Reaches under table for a*
17   *bottle.)* Oh, and you're going to want this.
18 WOMAN: Antacid?
19 VENDOR 2: We call it dessert. *(Woman exits. VENDOR 2 looks at*
20   *the audience.)* Hey, look at all the people out there!
21 VENDOR 1: Don't even think about it. These people are spirit-
22   filled, godly warriors. They would never think of
23   partaking in your unhealthy diet.
24 VENDOR 2: Then I'm taking the coffee pot. *(Grabs the coffee pot*
25   *off VENDOR 1's table and exits.)*
26 VENDOR 1: Hey, you don't have to be so cruel! *(Chases after*
27   *VENDOR 2.)*

Interview with a Grump

Theme
Choices

Scripture Reference
Matthew 16:26; John 12:25

Synopsis
A decorated soldier shares what is really important in life.

Cast
Reporter
Arnold

Props
Microphone for Reporter and cane for Arnold

Setting
A television studio. You may place two chairs at
Center Stage, or the characters may simply stand.

1   *(REPORTER and ARNOLD are in place at Center Stage.)*
2   REPORTER: Ladies and gentlemen, I'd like to introduce you to
3   the most decorated human being in this lifetime, Arnold
4   Mendenhall. *(To ARNOLD)* **Arnold, today you are one**
5   **hundred years old. Am I correct?**
6   ARNOLD: That is right.
7   REPORTER: You've seen a lot in your lifetime.
8   ARNOLD: I suppose.
9   REPORTER: You served in World War I and World War II, got
10   three medals for going above and beyond the line of duty,
11   one Purple Heart, and one Congressional Medal of Honor.
12   ARNOLD: That sounds about right.
13   REPORTER: You've seen great progress in your life, from the
14   simple one-engine planes to traveling in space.
15   ARNOLD: I guess.
16   REPORTER: You guess? Why, it's absolutely fantastic what
17   humankind has accomplished in this short lifespan, and
18   you've been a witness to it all.
19   ARNOLD: I suppose I have.
20   REPORTER: What do you make of all these changes?
21   ARNOLD: I was against it all.
22   REPORTER: *(Gasps.)* What? How can you say that?
23   ARNOLD: I never did like change much.
24   REPORTER: OK ... then tell me, what was the highlight of
25   your life?
26   ARNOLD: The 1940s.
27   REPORTER: Because we won the war? No, wait! I'll bet it was
28   because you met the president.
29   ARNOLD: Nope. Movies finally got some color in them. I hate
30   black and white.
31   REPORTER: Tell me then, what was your greatest
32   accomplishment?
33   ARNOLD: Getting out of bed this morning.
34   REPORTER: *(Starting to lose his enthusiasm)* Were you ever
35   married?
36   ARNOLD: Darn tootin'. I had me a lovely wife. We were

1   married for sixty-seven years.
2   REPORTER: That's incredible. What was her name?
3   ARNOLD: I don't remember.
4   REPORTER: Any children?
5   ARNOLD: Three girls, but don't ask me their names either. I
6   only remember the one named after me.
7   REPORTER: Uh … Arnelli?
8   ARNOLD: Nope, Junior.
9   REPORTER: So Arnold, do you remember when you dedicated
10   yourself to the Lord?
11   ARNOLD: Absolutely. A fellow doesn't forget an important
12   event like that.
13   REPORTER: So when was it?
14   ARNOLD: When was what?
15   REPORTER: The day you gave your life to Jesus.
16   ARNOLD: I don't remember.
17   REPORTER: But you just said …
18   ARNOLD: You asked if I recalled it. That I do. The exact day
19   escapes me.
20   REPORTER: So what were the exciting events that led you to
21   the Lord?
22   ARNOLD: My wife was responsible.
23   REPORTER: Oh, she was able to show the truth of the Word
24   through Scripture?
25   ARNOLD: Nope, she told me she was done praying for me. She
26   said she kept at it for forty years, and now I was on my
27   own.
28   REPORTER: Really?
29   ARNOLD: You know, that's enough to scare the beegeebees out
30   of most guys.
31   REPORTER: Why is that?
32   ARNOLD: Well if she wasn't going to pray for me, I figured I'd
33   better get on good terms with the Almighty myself.
34   REPORTER: Any regrets?
35   ARNOLD: Just one; that I didn't know the Lord sooner in my
36   life. It's hard to change when you're a grump like me.

1   REPORTER: You don't seem too grumpy to me.
2   ARNOLD: No, not grump, G-R-U-M-P! It stands for God
3   Reconstructing Under Man's Protest.
4   REPORTER: Oh, I see.
5   ARNOLD: Yes, there's a lot of G.R.U.M.P.s like me out there.
6   We kind of like the way things are, so we cruise around
7   life, and *bam!*
8   REPORTER: Bam?
9   ARNOLD: The easy ride stops, and you have to take
10   responsibility for your relationship with the Lord. *(Pause)*
11   You have no idea how hard it is for us G.R.U.M.P.s to
12   change.
13   REPORTER: Sometimes change is a good thing.
14   ARNOLD: Yes, but for us G.R.U.M.P.s, we need extra
15   motivation. We need the gentle prodding of a baseball bat
16   to the back of the head before we accept change.
17   REPORTER: What happens when it finally hits the mark?
18   ARNOLD: You realize that progress isn't really that big of a
19   deal. A man's true progress starts when he believes in
20   Jesus.
21   REPORTER: I'll bet your wife was pleased when you told her
22   that.
23   ARNOLD: *(Shakes his head.)* Never told her.
24   REPORTER: What? All those years she prayed for you, and you
25   never once let her know what the Lord meant to you?
26   ARNOLD: That's right.
27   REPORTER: But why?
28   ARNOLD: Sixty-seven years of thinking her husband is
29   damned for all eternity ... Why ruin a good run?
30   REPORTER: You really are a grump.

It's All in the Translation

Theme
The Lord's Prayer

Scripture Reference
Matthew 6:7-14

Synopsis
The Lord's Prayer with a slightly different twist.

Cast
Pastor
Stu Mulligan

Props
None

Setting
A worship service

1   *(PASTOR is in place at the pulpit.)*
2   PASTOR: I understand we have some newcomers here today.
3   While our older members are used to our way of praying,
4   some of our newer members have expressed that they are
5   having trouble interpreting what we're actually saying.
6   So to solve the problem, we've hired an interpreter. May I
7   present Stu Mulligan. *(STU enters and gives the audience a*
8   *double thumbs-up.)* Let us pray. *(Clears his throat.)* Our Father
9   who art in heaven, hallowed be thy name.
10   STU: Yo God, your name rocks! *(Raises a fist for emphasis.)*
11   PASTOR: Thy kingdom come. Thy will be done on earth, as it
12   is in heaven.
13   STU: Whatever you want me to do, Lord, I'm there for ya.
14   PASTOR: Give us this day our daily bread.
15   STU: Food, clothes, I'm good, man.
16   PASTOR: And forgive us our trespasses ... *(Or "debts," if your*
17   *congregation prefers.)*
18   STU: Thanks for not holding it over my head when I mess up.
19   PASTOR: As we forgive those who trespass against us. *(Or*
20   *"debtors.")*
21   STU: Hey, if you can be the better man, so can I.
22   PASTOR: And lead us not into temptation, but deliver us from
23   evil.
24   STU: Keep me away from the bad dudes, Lord.
25   PASTOR: For thine is the kingdom ...
26   STU: You rule!
27   PASTOR: And the power ...
28   STU: Major mojo!
29   PASTOR: and the glory ...
30   STU: You rock, man!
31   PASTOR: For ever and ever.
32   STU: Until the end of time ... or longer.
33   PASTOR: Amen.
34   STU: *(Claps hands together and hold them out, palms toward the*
35   *audience.)* I'm done.
36   PASTOR: Thank you, Stu. That was very helpful.

1   STU: Any time, man.

2   PASTOR: I'm curious — what do you say when you ask God

3   for assistance in a certain area of your life?

4   STU: I don't understand.

5   PASTOR: I mean, whenever you have a need or you're in pain,

6   what do you say?

7   STU: Oh, that! *(Raises hands in the air.)* Heeeelp!

8   PASTOR: Simple, yet effective.

Keep It Simple

Theme
Prayer

Scripture Reference
Matthew 6:5-8

Synopsis
A member just wants to pray, but keeps getting interrupted and instructed on technique.

Cast
Brad
Charles
Denise

Props
None

Setting
Nonspecific

1   *(BRAD enters and stands at Center Stage. CHARLES follows*
2   *soon after.)*
3   **BRAD: Dear God —**
4   **CHARLES: What are you doing?**
5   **BRAD: What? I'm praying.**
6   **CHARLES: You're doing it all wrong! You're supposed to kneel**
7   **when you pray.**
8   **BRAD: I am?**
9   **CHARLES: Absolutely. Go ahead and try it.**
10   **BRAD:** *(Kneels.)* **Dear God —** *(DENISE enters.)*
11   **DENISE: Hold it. You're doing it wrong.**
12   **BRAD: I'm doing** *what* **wrong?**
13   **DENISE: You're supposed to put the palms of your hands**
14   **together like this.** *(Shows traditional palm to palm hand*
15   *position.)*
16   **CHARLES: People don't do that anymore. You're supposed to**
17   **intertwine your fingers like this.** *(Demonstrates.)*
18   **DENISE: Palms together shows a more reverent stance.**
19   **CHARLES: But fingers intertwined shows a more humbling**
20   **stance.**
21   **BRAD:** *(Standing)* **Look, I just wanted to say a simple prayer to**
22   **God.**
23   **CHARLES: Kneel!** *(BRAD quickly returns to a kneeling position.)*
24   **DENISE: You don't have to be so old school. It's perfectly**
25   **acceptable to sit when you pray.**
26   **BRAD: Sitting would be much more comfortable.**
27   **CHARLES: Prayer isn't as effective unless there's some real**
28   **pain behind it.**
29   **DENISE: Where did you come up with that baloney?**
30   **CHARLES: Everyone knows you come to prayer with a humble**
31   **spirit and a contrite heart.**
32   **DENISE: In attitude. The position doesn't matter.**
33   **BRAD: Oh, good. I'll stand then.** *(Starts to get up, but CHARLES*
34   *pushes him down.)* **Then again, maybe I won't.**
35   **CHARLES: Now don't forget the "thees" and "thous" when**
36   **you pray.**

1 DENISE: Don't be silly. You don't have to use King James
2   language. Just say what's on your mind.
3 CHARLES: But it must be expressed in an appropriate manner.
4   For example: "Thou art the mightiest in the heavens, O
5   Lord. Thy will is in perfect accord with thy Spirit."
6 DENISE: OK, take that prayer and simplify it to, "Not by my
7   will, but your will, God."
8 BRAD: Actually, my prayer is very simple. I just want to say —
9 CHARLES: Quiet. This is very important.
10 DENISE: Didn't your mother tell you it's rude to interrupt?
11 BRAD: Sorry.
12 DENISE: Now where were we?
13 BRAD: I was trying to pray, and you two came in.
14 DENISE: That's right. Go ahead.
15 BRAD: Right now? In front of everyone? *(Eyes shift from*
16   *DENISE to CHARLES through the following exchange.)*
17 CHARLES: Of course. A prayer doesn't count unless it's said
18   out in the open.
19 DENISE: If you're a Pharisee, God says to pray in private.
20 CHARLES: Paul said to pray with other believers.
21 DENISE: But he doesn't want you to be a hypocrite.
22 CHARLES: You have to be sincere.
23 DENISE: And it has to come from the heart.
24 CHARLES: If you think about it, it's a sacred path of
25   communication between you and the Almighty.
26 DENISE: That's right, so don't mess it up.
27 BRAD: *(When DENISE and CHARLES finally stop talking, BRAD*
28   *pauses, making several attempts to start a prayer, but stops short,*
29   *glancing from one to another. The longer the pause, the funnier it*
30   *becomes.)* **Dear God, help!**
31 CHARLES: That pretty much says it all.
32 DENISE: It does sum it up nicely.
33 CHARLES: Nice and simple.
34 DENISE: But direct and to the point.
35 CHARLES: Exactly. *(They exit leaving BRAD alone. He stands,*
36   *shrugs, and exits.)*

Marriage Counselor

Theme
Anger

Scripture Reference
Psalm 15:1; Proverbs 17:14, 30:33; Ephesians 4:3;
Colossians 3:18

Synopsis
A husband and wife have "issues."

Cast
Husband
Wife
Counselor

Props
None

Setting
The Counselor's office. One small table or desk
with chair is positioned at Center Stage and two
chairs are off to the side.

1   *(WIFE enters with HUSBAND.)*
2   WIFE: I can't believe you're so stupid. Why do I bother taking
3   you anywhere?
4   HUSBAND: We would have gotten here sooner if you hadn't
5   insisted on turning right at Alcove Street. *(COUNSELOR*
6   *enters and sits at desk.)*
7   WIFE: I didn't say "right," I said "*left.*"
8   HUSBAND: I asked you if we needed to turn left, but you said
9   "right."
10   WIFE: I wasn't giving you directions, I was agreeing with you.
11   HUSBAND: That's a first.
12   WIFE: *(Accusing)* What do you mean by that?!
13   COUNSELOR: Whoa — hang on there. Remember what I told
14   you on the phone? No arguing *until* you get to the
15   counseling center. *(HUSBAND and WIFE sit.)*
16   HUSBAND: *(Points at WIFE.)* She started it.
17   COUNSELOR: Pointing fingers is not acceptable either.
18   WIFE: *(Smug)* Ha, ha.
19   COUNSELOR: Derogatory expressions are also not allowed.
20   You see, at the Quick Stop Counseling Center, we have
21   one surefire way to solve a conflict between husbands
22   and wives.
23   HUSBAND: For two hundred dollars an hour, it had better be
24   good. *(Turns to WIFE.)* I can't believe we're spending this
25   much.
26   WIFE: Put a crowbar in your pocket and dish it out for a
27   change.
28   COUNSELOR: It looks like I'm going to have to bring in the
29   big guns right away. There's no wasting time when it
30   comes to you two.
31   HUSBAND: *(Hopeful)* We're using guns?
32   COUNSELOR: It's just a figure of speech.
33   HUSBAND: *(Disappointed)* Oh. Bummer.
34   WIFE: Let's get on with it, shall we? We have some furniture to
35   move today.
36   HUSBAND: No, we don't, *(Strained)* dear.

1   WIFE: Yes, we do, *(Strained)* sweetheart.

2   COUNSELOR: There. You see? You've just stepped in the door,

3   and you're already starting to get along. We just have to do

4   one thing and we'll call this problem resolved.

5   *(COUNSELOR takes two chairs and places them facing each*

6   *other at the table.)*

7   HUSBAND: Are we going to sit and talk? That never works.

8   WIFE: That's because you never listen to my side.

9   HUSBAND: That's because you never have anything worth

10   listening to.

11   COUNSELOR: Now, now, personal badgering won't be

12   allowed. We've set up a completely fair problem-solving

13   situation, but there are certain rules you must follow.

14   HUSBAND: Such as?

15   COUNSELOR: No insults, no gestures like the rolling of the

16   eyes, *(Shows exaggerated gesture)* no derogatory remarks,

17   and no cheating.

18   WIFE: How can you cheat at a counseling center?

19   COUNSELOR: Because I'm not going to counsel you. You're

20   going to resolve this on your own.

21   HUSBAND: How?

22   COUNSELOR: You're going to arm wrestle.

23   HUSBAND and WIFE: What?!

24   COUNSELOR: You're going to sit opposite each other and arm

25   wrestle for your right to have your way.

26   WIFE: This is insane.

27   COUNSELOR: Oh, it's entirely biblical.

28   WIFE: How?

29   COUNSELOR: Jacob wrestled with God all night. The prize

30   was a blessing. So arm wrestling is purely Scriptural in a

31   much less violent sort of way.

32   HUSBAND: So how is this going to help us — in a nonviolent

33   sort of way?

34   COUNSELOR: It's easy. Winner takes all, and the loser has to

35   humbly "eat crow" and agree to the other's demands. Are

36   we ready?

1 HUSBAND: Ready. *(To audience)* **This will be a piece of cake.**

2 WIFE: **This hardly seems fair. He's bigger than I am.**

3 HUSBAND: **What's the matter,** *(Strained)* **dear — afraid to back**

4 **up your words with action?**

5 WIFE: *(To COUNSELOR)* **Move over.** *(BOTH sit opposite each other*

6 *and clasp hands. COUNSELOR places both hands over*

7 *HUSBAND and WIFE.)*

8 COUNSELOR: **Now, once I let go, the contest is on. The loser**

9 **agrees to abide by the winner's decision. Are you ready?**

10 HUSBAND: **Bring it on.**

11 WIFE: **You're toast.**

12 HUSBAND: **Takes one to know one, milk sop.**

13 COUNSELOR: **Ah-ah-ah, no derogatory remarks. It's now time**

14 **to settle. Go!** *(COUNSELOR lets go and they BOTH start to*

15 *struggle, first going his way, then her way.)*

16 HUSBAND: **Are you ready to give up now?**

17 WIFE: **You wish.**

18 HUSBAND: **I can't believe you're making me do this.**

19 WIFE: **Making you? You're the one who won't listen to reason.**

20 HUSBAND: **That's because you're unreasonable.**

21 COUNSELOR: **Check bitterness at the door. Ephesians 4:31**

22 **says to get rid of all bitterness, anger, brawling, and**

23 **malice** *(Author's paraphrase).*

24 HUSBAND: **Then** *she* **won't have any personality left. Whoa!**

25 *(WIFE almost overtakes him. He struggles to get back to center.)*

26 COUNSELOR: **No stirring up more anger. Scripture says,**

27 **"Surely the churning of milk bringeth forth butter, and**

28 **the wringing of the nose bringeth forth blood; so the**

29 **forcing of wrath bringeth forth strife"** *(Proverbs 30:33,*

30 *KJV).*

31 HUSBAND: **As long as you're quoting Scripture, you forgot**

32 **the part that says she's supposed to obey my every**

33 **command.**

34 WIFE: **Ha! What about the part where it says to love your wife**

35 **and don't complain when she goes to the mall?**

36 COUNSELOR: **Foul! No misquoting Scripture. Stick to the**

1   anger issues.

2   **WIFE: You know, you're really cute when you struggle.**

3   **HUSBAND:** *(Looks up, surprised.)* **What?** *(WIFE takes advantage of*

4   *his momentary weakness and slams his hand down in victory.)*

5   **COUNSELOR: Beaten with Psalm 15:1! "A soft answer will**

6   **turn away wrath"** *(Author's paraphrase).* **It's settled, then.**

7   *(COUNSELOR places her hands on HUSBAND's shoulders.)*

8   **The mother-in-law moves in.**

9   **WIFE:** *(Jumps up and raises her arms in victory.)* **Yes!** *(HUSBAND*

10   *hangs his head and cries.)*

Mouse Trap

Theme
Temptation

Scripture Reference
Psalm 91:3; 1 Corinthians 10:13

Synopsis
A father discusses the dangers of entrapment.

Cast
Dad
Freddie

Props
None

Setting
At home

1   (*DAD is crouched down on the floor. FREDDIE enters.*)
2   FREDDIE: Hi, Dad!
3   DAD: Shhhh.
4   FREDDIE: What are you doing?
5   DAD: I'm waiting for the mouse to come out of the hole.
6   FREDDIE: Why are you doing that?
7   DAD: So we can catch it.
8   FREDDIE: Oh, goody! Can I sleep with it tonight?
9   DAD: We're not going to keep it as a pet. I'm waiting to see if
10   it takes the bait.
11   FREDDIE: What's bait, Dad?
12   DAD: Well, you get something the little rodent loves to eat, like
13   cheese ...
14   FREDDIE: I like cheese too.
15   DAD: Then you place the cheese on a trap.
16   FREDDIE: That wooden thing with the spring?
17   DAD: That's right. As the mouse tries to take the cheese, he sets
18   off the spring, it snaps his neck, and it's "bye-bye,
19   mouse."
20   FREDDIE: So you use something the mouse wants to try to trap
21   it and kill it?
22   DAD: That's right.
23   FREDDIE: But that seems so unfair.
24   DAD: It's no different from what Satan does to us.
25   FREDDIE: Really?!
26   DAD: Sure. The Bible is full of stories of Satan trapping godly
27   men using their weaknesses. Take the story of Samson, for
28   example. His weakness was his desire for a woman
29   named Delilah.
30   FREDDIE: What'd he do?
31   DAD: He gave away the secret of his strength. Then there was
32   King David. His weakness was this woman named
33   Bathsheba. He had her husband killed so he could marry
34   her.
35   FREDDIE: Wow!
36   DAD: And then there was King Solomon. His weakness was

1   this one pagan wife who convinced him to make her a
2   place to worship her false gods. After a time, even *he*
3   started worshiping those gods and lost favor with the one
4   true God.
5   FREDDIE: For a smart guy, Solomon was kinda stupid.
6   DAD: It was a poor choice in that instant. Sort of makes you
7   think, doesn't it?
8   FREDDIE: Yeah. *(Pause)* Stay away from girls.
9   DAD: No, Freddie, that's not the point I was trying to make.
10 FREDDIE: I've always thought they're kind of creepy.
11 DAD: Listen to me —
12 FREDDIE: The way they put things in their hair, they look at
13   you with googly eyes and then giggle ... What's with
14   that?!
15 DAD: Uh, well, they're a little different from us.
16 FREDDIE: You're telling me! And the Bible is full of warnings
17   to keep away.
18 DAD: *(Turns to audience.)* How did this get away from me?
19 FREDDIE: Dresses and lace and dolls ... no normal person
20   likes those!
21 DAD: Freddie, it wasn't the woman herself causing the
22   weakness, it was the man's *desire* for the woman.
23 FREDDIE: Oh. So they actually wanted to hang around with
24   girls? Boy, did they have their priorities mixed up!
25 DAD: Sometimes temptation does that too.
26 FREDDIE: So then, the girls were the cheese!
27 DAD: I never thought of it that way, but you're right. *(Pause)*
28   Well, shall we go have some lunch?
29 FREDDIE: What are we having?
30 DAD: Cheese pizza.
31 FREDDIE: *(Running Off-stage)* Mom! Dad's trying to trap me!

My Way

Theme
Legalism

Scripture Reference
Romans 7:1-4; Ephesians 4:6

Synopsis
One person takes another on a joy ride, only to find
it's a lot more work than anticipated.

Cast
Lucy
Edward

Props
None

Setting
Two chairs facing the audience may represent a car,
with an optional steering wheel for effect (or the actor
may mime driving).

1   (*LUCY is seated in the "driver's seat." EDWARD enters.*)
2   EDWARD: Hi, Lucy. What are you doing?
3   LUCY: I'm getting ready to hit the road of life. Would you like
4   to come with me?
5   EDWARD: I'm actually doing quite well. I have my own car for
6   the road of life.
7   LUCY: What kind of a car is it?
8   EDWARD: Just a basic four-door sedan.
9   LUCY: Ha. I have a red sports car with black leather interior.
10   Beautiful, isn't it?
11   EDWARD: Very flashy.
12   LUCY: And very chic. This little baby can get from one to sixty
13   in four seconds. Come with me.
14   EDWARD: Well, I really shouldn't, but I can't resist.
15   LUCY: OK, then. (*EDWARD gets in the passenger side. LUCY sits*
16   *in the driver's side at first, then gets out and starts to push.*)
17   EDWARD: What are you doing?
18   LUCY: What does it look like I'm doing? I'm pushing.
19   EDWARD: Why are you pushing?
20   LUCY: It certainly can't go all by itself. Hey, is the parking
21   brake released?
22   EDWARD: Yes, it is. But did you know you also have a full
23   tank of gas?
24   LUCY: I prefer to drive this on my own. I don't need any help.
25   EDWARD: But it's already here for you to use.
26   LUCY: Are you gonna just sit there, or are you going to help
27   me?
28   EDWARD: (*Getting out*) It sure seems like a lot more work than
29   necessary. (*They push and grunt.*) Why don't we just turn
30   the engine on?
31   LUCY: (*Grunting*) I told you, I like doing things on my own.
32   Hey, we're at the top of the hill. Get in quick. (*They both*
33   *quickly get into the car.*) Wheeee! See? I told you this was
34   fun. Hang on — we're really going fast now!
35   EDWARD: We're slowing down.
36   LUCY: Oh, bother. OK, let's get out and push again.

1   EDWARD: Are you crazy? Do you see how big that hill is?

2   LUCY: Yeah. We're gonna have to push harder. Let's go.

3   EDWARD: No way. *(He gets out.)* My car may not be flashy or

4   beautiful in appearance, but it was given to me to drive. I

5   don't need to push it because the gas was given to me as a

6   free gift to help me on my journey.

7   LUCY: Fine! You just coast through life with your free gas.

8   When I get to where I'm going, at least I'll be able to say I

9   did it myself.

10 EDWARD: If you get there at all. Hey, your engine is smoking.

11   Did you check your oil before you left?

12 LUCY: Cars have oil? *(They exit.)*

No More Excuses

Theme
God's calling, the excuses we make

Scripture Reference
Exodus 3

Synopsis
When God wants Moses to go into Egypt to free his people, Moses offers alternative solutions.

Cast
God (Off-stage God)
Moses
Narrator

Costumes
Biblical robe for Moses

Props
None

Setting
On Mount Horeb in biblical times.

1   (*NARRATOR and MOSES enter.*)
2   NARRATOR: In Bible study, we learn about many interesting
3   characters. For example, Moses became one of the greatest
4   prophets in the Old Testament. He shows us his depth of
5   character, unwavering faith, and unfailing courage.
6   MOSES: (*Looks surprised at NARRATOR.*) Are you talking about
7   me?
8   NARRATOR: It all began when he heard the call from God.
9   MOSES: What call? I was only checking out the burning bush.
10   GOD: (*All GOD's lines are said from Off-stage.*) Moses.
11   MOSES: Whoa. Who said that?
12   GOD: I am the God of Abraham, the God of Isaac, and the God
13   of Jacob.
14   MOSES: No kidding? Are there any more in there?
15   GOD: I am sending you on a great mission. I want you to free
16   the slaves in Egypt.
17   MOSES: I-I can't do that. Pharaoh will have me executed.
18   GOD: I will protect you every step of the way.
19   MOSES: But I have no weapons. No army!
20   GOD: When you go to Pharaoh, throw down your staff. I will
21   turn it into a scorpion.
22   MOSES: No scorpions. I hate those little creatures.
23   GOD: A lizard, then.
24   MOSES: Yeah, right. You grab the tail, and they just keep on
25   running.
26   GOD: A snake.
27   MOSES: That whole tongue thing really freaks me out.
28   GOD: Then I will send you with nothing.
29   MOSES: Snake is good! A snake works for me.
30   GOD: When you reach Pharoah's court, present the staff and
31   demand the release of my people.
32   MOSES: (*Shakes his head.*) No can do. I can't talk.
33   GOD: What do you mean, you can't talk?
34   MOSES: I have a real bad stuttering problem. I can hardly say
35   two words coherently in one sentence.
36   GOD: What stuttering problem?

1 MOSES: *(Caught off-guard. Pauses for effect.)* I-I m-mean ... I
2   c-can't t-t-talk v-very g-g-good.
3 GOD: Save it, Moses. You don't have to speak to Ramsey.
4   *(MOSES sighs.)* Your brother Aaron will do it.
5 MOSES: I have a brother? Why can't he do it? After all, we're
6   part of the same gene pool. Besides, what will we do after
7   all the people are set free?
8 GOD: You will lead my people to a place where I will give
9   them the fifteen commandments.
10 MOSES: Fifteen? That's a bit much, don't you think? Besides,
11   most of these people can't even read! How about five
12   commandments?
13 GOD: Ten commandments.
14 MOSES: How about seven? That's a nice even number.
15 GOD: How about we leave the people in slavery?
16 MOSES: Ten is good. Ten works for me.
17 GOD: Now, go and free my people.
18 MOSES: Can't I do this next year? This really isn't a good time
19   for me. The sheep have been sick, and my wife wants new
20   curtains for the tent. Besides, it's not even the weekend!
21 GOD: Moses, have you noticed that the bush burns, but it's not
22   actually on fire?
23 MOSES: Yes.
24 GOD: I can do the same to people.
25 MOSES: *(Quickly)* Today is good! Today works for me. *(Starts to*
26   *exit.)* Although the desert is really hot this time of year,
27   and the camels tend to spit more when they're overheated
28   ... *(Turns back to bush.)* But I don't mind. I'll be there.
29   *(Exits.)*
30 NARRATOR: So what's your excuse? Don't wait for God to call
31   you from a burning bush.

One and the Same

Theme
Marriage

Scripture Reference
Proverbs 18:22

Synopsis
An older couple discusses the success of their years together.

Cast
Norman
Rae Lyn

Props
None

Setting
Nonspecific

1 (*NORMAN and RAE LYN stand at Center Stage.*)
2 NORMAN: (*Introducing themselves*) **Hello, my name is Norman,**
3 **and this is my wife, Rae Lyn. You know, people marvel**
4 **when I tell them how long we've been married.**
5 RAE LYN: **But in our day, it was expected that couples would**
6 **try to stick it out.**
7 NORMAN: **Sometimes the glue got sticky.**
8 RAE LYN: **Sometimes the glue got old.**
9 NORMAN: **For better or for worse —**
10 RAE LYN: **And there was plenty of worse.**
11 NORMAN: **But what held us together were all the things we**
12 **have in common. For example, I like action movies.**
13 RAE LYN: **I like romance.**
14 NORMAN: **I read textbooks.**
15 RAE LYN: **I read novels.**
16 NORMAN: **I like to watch TV.**
17 RAE LYN: **I like to sit and talk.**
18 NORMAN: **I avoid conversation.**
19 RAE LYN: **I can speak on five different subjects at the same**
20 **time.**
21 NORMAN: **As you can see, we were made for each other. I'll**
22 **never forget the first day she made me dinner. It was**
23 **delicious — except for the fact that I prefer my peanut**
24 **butter crunchy.**
25 RAE LYN: **I like it creamy.**
26 NORMAN: **And I prefer it on white bread.**
27 RAE LYN: **Whole grain is better for you.**
28 NORMAN: **I like it with whole milk.**
29 RAE LYN: **I drink skim.**
30 NORMAN: **Pepsi is my first choice for soda.**
31 RAE LYN: **I prefer Coke.**
32 NORMAN: **A nice thick steak for dinner.**
33 RAE LYN: **A small piece of fish.**
34 NORMAN: **Yes, we're similar in many ways. Then we started**
35 **our family. I wanted two.**
36 RAE LYN: **I wanted five.**

1   NORMAN: I definitely wanted two.
2   RAE LYN: I wanted five.
3   NORMAN: I said I'd consider three.
4   RAE LYN: I wanted five.
5   NORMAN: Four, and I was putting my foot down.
6   RAE LYN: I wanted five.
7   NORMAN: We had five. *(Pause)* Of course, we were always in
8   agreement when it came to raising the children. I believed
9   in a strong hand.
10 RAE LYN: I believed in gentle instruction.
11 NORMAN: "Foolishness is bound in the heart of a child; but
12   the rod of correction shall drive it from him" *(Proverbs*
13   *22:5).*
14 RAE LYN: "A soft answer will turn away wrath" *(Proverbs 5:1).*
15 NORMAN: But as the kids grew up, we were adamant that they
16   go to college.
17 RAE LYN: I was happy just to get them through high school.
18 NORMAN: Happiness is a higher education
19 RAE LYN: Happiness is finding your place with the Lord.
20 NORMAN: You see how we fit?
21 RAE LYN: Like two pieces of a puzzle.
22 NORMAN: "Whosoever finds a wife finds a good thing, and
23   obtains the favor of the Lord" *(Proverbs 8:22).*
24 RAE LYN: That's the truth.
25 NORMAN: Uh, aren't you going to reciprocate with a passage
26   about husbands?
27 RAE LYN: No, I think that says it all.
28 NORMAN: And finally to you husbands, the success to years
29   of happiness is to always remember those three important
30   little words.
31 RAE LYN: "Where's the remote?"
32 NORMAN: No.
33 RAE LYN: "I love you"?
34 NORMAN: No. "I was wrong."
35 RAE LYN: Now *that's* the wisdom of Solomon.

The Path of Most Resistance

Theme
Retirement, the road of life

Scripture Reference
John 10:10

Synopsis
A group walking on the road of life learns what it means to "travel light."

Cast
Guide
Roy
Mabel
Walter
Gladys
Ethel

Props
Two binoculars, two remote controls, two bags (one for Ethel and one for Gladys), hand-sized rocks, one brick, a shoulder pad, and a small pillow

Setting
Outside, on the road of life. You will need a folding chair.

1   *(The GUIDE enters with ALL following behind. He stops*
2   *midstage.)*
3   **GUIDE: Look, everyone.** *(Extends his/her arm toward the audience.)*
4   **The final stretch on the road of life.** *(All move forward and*
5   *peer out over the audience.)*
6   **MABEL:** *(Skeptical)* **This is it?**
7   **GLADYS: It's beautiful. Look at the sunset.**
8   **MABEL: Is** *that* **what the young women are wearing in the**
9   **future? Why, it's positively indecent.**
10   **ROY:** *(Approvingly)* **Yeaaaah.** *(MABEL backhands him on his*
11   *shoulder. ROY quickly responds.)* **I mean — terrible.**
12   **ETHEL: Has anyone seen Walter?** *(From behind, WALTER crashes*
13   *into everyone as he is walking backward with binoculars. He looks*
14   *everywhere except forward for the whole performance.)*
15   **ALL:** *(Ad-lib responses, all speaking at the same time.)* **Ouch! Watch**
16   **it! Aargh! Oof.**
17   **GUIDE: For goodness sake, Walter, turn around and watch**
18   **where you're going.**
19   **WALTER: Are you kidding? I invested a good deal of my life**
20   **back there.**
21   **GLADYS: But there's so much to see up ahead.** *(To GUIDE)* **Is it**
22   **really as smooth as it looks?**
23   **GUIDE: There are still some bumps in the road, but the hard**
24   **climb is over. The kids are grown ...** *(ALL nod in consent.)*
25   **WALTER: Never thought we'd get them out of the house.**
26   **GUIDE: The mortgage is paid ...** *(Some nod, others rock hands in a*
27   *"so-so" motion.)* **And now, the golden years of retirement**
28   **await us.**
29   **ROY: Thought that would never happen.** *(He pulls out a chair and*
30   *sits.)*
31   **MABEL: What are you doing?**
32   **ROY: I'm retiring.**
33   **MABEL: Right here? I thought we were going to walk this road**
34   **together.**
35   **ROY:** *(Looking on the ground)* **Where's the remote?** *(GLADYS*
36   *hands a remote to ROY.)*

1 MABEL: If you'd just look at the sunrise, you'd see how
2   beautiful the future is.
3 WALTER: *(Pulls his binoculars away just enough to talk to ROY.)*
4   Don't do it, Roy. Take my advice — it was a lot better
5   where we came from.
6 GUIDE: How can you say that? You still have a rich, fulfilling
7   life ahead of you.
8 WALTER: I'm perfectly happy where I am, thanks.
9 ROY: So am I.
10 GUIDE: There are so many possibilities over there. .
11   volunteering for charities, sharing the wisdom of your
12   experiences ...
13 MABEL: Evening strolls at sunset ...
14 GLADYS: Helping in the community ...
15 WALTER: As riveting as that sounds, I've got other things to
16   concentrate on. *(Points Off-stage while still looking through*
17   *binoculars.)*
18 WALTER: That's when I lost my job, and there's when the bank
19   took my home. Oh, and look, there's the time my first
20   wife left me.
21 ROY: Believe me, my friend, that was one of your better
22   moments.
23 GUIDE: Ready to go, Ethel?
24 ETHEL: *(Nervously clutches her handbag.)* Oh, I can't. Thank you
25   for bringing me this far, but I just don't think I'm capable
26   of going any farther.
27 GUIDE: Why not?
28 ETHEL: Well, what if they don't like me? What if I can't
29   measure up to their expectations? I mean, I don't even
30   own a computer.
31 ROY: All that computer stuff is overrated. Why, most of these
32   fancy doo-dads are a waste of time and money. *(Plays with*
33   *the remote, then turns to GUIDE.)* Does this have surround
34   sound?
35 WALTER: In our day, we used our imagination.
36 GUIDE: Yes, but look at all the new and exciting things you're

1   going to learn.

2   **ETHEL: But what if I fail? What if they tell me I'm no good? I**

3   **just don't think I can handle that kind of rejection.** *(As*

4   *ETHEL talks, GLADYS hands her stones that she puts in her*

5   *purse.)*

6   **GUIDE: Um ... Ethel? What are you doing?**

7   **ETHEL: What do you mean?**

8   **GUIDE: Why are you putting rocks in your purse?**

9   **ETHEL: These aren't ordinary rocks. These are my worries.**

10   **GUIDE:** *(Looks inside purse.)* **That's a lot of worries.**

11   **WALTER: This is nothing. She's got canisters full of them back**

12   **home.**

13   **ETHEL: I like to keep myself supplied at all times.**

14   **GUIDE: But doesn't that get sort of heavy?**

15   **ETHEL: Oh, yes. In fact, sometimes the weight is so intense it**

16   **hurts my shoulder.** *(GLADYS puts a shoulder pad on her*

17   *shoulder.)* **Thank you, Gladys.**

18   **GUIDE:** *(To GLADYS)* **And what are you doing?**

19   **GLADYS:** *(Cheerfully)* **Just helping.**

20   **WALTER: My binoculars just broke.**

21   **GLADYS: Here you go, Walter. I always carry a spare.**

22   **WALTER: Thank you, Gladys.** *(Accidentally looks toward the*

23   *audience and yelps in horror. GLADYS turns him around, facing*

24   *Off-stage again.)* **Ahhhh. That's much better.**

25   **ROY: You wouldn't happen to have a seat cushion, would you?**

26   *(GLADYS hands him a small pillow.)*

27   **MABEL: Thanks a lot. How am I ever going to move him now?**

28   **ETHEL: I should do something. What could I do?** *(GLADYS*

29   *takes a brick and plunks it in ETHEL's purse. ETHEL reacts with*

30   *a jerk.)* **That should keep me occupied.**

31   **GUIDE: Hold it, everybody!** *(ALL cast looks at GUIDE.)* **If we're**

32   **going to have a successful journey, the first thing we have**

33   **to do is drop the baggage.**

34   **ETHEL: I beg your pardon?**

35   **GUIDE: Get rid of all the stuff that's holding you down. These**

36   **can be our most productive years, but you can't enter them**

1 **by** *(Goes to WALTER and takes away the binoculars)* **hanging**
2 **on to the past ...**
3 WALTER: Hey!
4 GUIDE: *(Goes over to ETHEL and takes her bag.)* **Worrying about**
5 **what others think of you ...**
6 ETHEL: But I *need* those.
7 GUIDE: *(Walks over to GLADYS.)* **Allowing others to bring you**
8 **down ...**
9 GLADYS: You can't possibly be referring to me!
10 GUIDE: *(Walks over to ROY.)* **And finally —**
11 ROY: Touch my chair, and you die! *(MABEL grabs his remote.)*
12 Now *that's* not fair.
13 GUIDE: This is the time we can all serve the Lord with our
14 whole heart. I don't know about the rest of you, but I've
15 been waiting for this all my life. Let's enter this valley
16 with our eyes not on our stuff, but on Christ. Who's with
17 me?
18 GLADYS: Oh, I am!
19 ETHEL: Me too. Come on, Walter. *(She grabs WALTER's arm and*
20 *begins to lead him Off-stage.)*
21 WALTER: I don't know. It's kind of weird walking forward.
22 ETHEL: It's lighter without my bag, too. *(ETHEL, WALTER, and*
23 *GLADYS exit.)*
24 GUIDE: *(To MABEL and ROY)* **Are you two coming?**
25 MABEL: *(At the same time with ROY)* **Yes ... yes ... yes.**
26 ROY: *(At the same time with MABEL)* **No ... no ... no.**
27 MABEL: Yes, I'm coming. *(Turns to ROY.)* **And so are you.**
28 ROY: Yes. *(ROY folds his chair, and he and MABEL exit, leaving the*
29 *GUIDE to stand alone on the stage.)*
30 GUIDE: Man, I thought I'd never get them off that mountain.
31 *(If the GUIDE is younger than the cast, add: "And they think*
32 *my generation is tough.")*

Pharisee Cleanser

Theme
Hypocrisy

Scripture Reference
Matthew 23:25-28

Synopsis
A dirty Pharisee? Something must be done.

Cast
Amos
Haddai
Spokeswoman
Sadducee

Costumes
Two white robes, one dirty robe, tassels, head coverings.
Sadducee's outfit is not as dirty as Haggai's outfit.

Props
Empty paint can with the words "Pharisee Cleanser"
on the outside, paint brush. You will need a table for the
Spokeswoman.

Setting
A street in Jerusalem.

1   *(SPOKESWOMAN is in place behind her table. AMOS stands*
2   *at Center Stage in a clean white robe. HAGGAI runs Onstage in*
3   *his dirty and tattered robe.)*
4   **HAGGAI: Amos, you've got to help me!**
5   **AMOS:** *(Pulls his arm away when HAGGAI touches him.)* **Be gone,**
6   **filthy scum, or I will call the authorities and have you**
7   **removed.**
8   **HAGGAI: Amos, it's me! It's Haggai.**
9   **AMOS: Haggai? For the love of Job, what happened to you?**
10   **HAGGAI: I-I don't know. I woke up this morning and I was**
11   **covered in filth. All my beautiful Pharisee clothing was**
12   **ripped to shreds.**
13   **AMOS: This is bad.**
14   **HAGGAI: I know. What am I going to do?**
15   **AMOS: No, I mean it's bad that someone might see me hanging**
16   **out with you. Go away before anyone notices.**
17   **HAGGAI: Please, Amos — you've got to help me. I'll lose my**
18   **place of importance among the Sanhedrin if they see me**
19   **like this.**
20   **AMOS: Oh, all right. I'll take you someplace, but you have to**
21   **promise not to tell a soul what you are about to see.**
22   **HAGGAI: I swear on my firstborn's life —**
23   **AMOS:** *(Cuts him off.)* **Save it. No one likes your kid anyway.**
24   **Come on.** *(AMOS leads HAGGAI across the stage to*
25   *SPOKESWOMAN behind a table.)*
26   **SPOKESWOMAN: Amos! So nice to see you. I wasn't**
27   **expecting you so soon after your last treatment —**
28   **AMOS: Keep it down! I'm not here for me, I'm here for a**
29   **friend.**
30   **WOMAN: Oh, I see. He does look like something the cat drug**
31   **in.**
32   **HAGGAI: Who are you?**
33   **AMOS and SPOKESWOMAN:** *(Together)* **Shhhh.**
34   **AMOS: If you're going to ask a lot of stupid questions, I'll take**
35   **you back where I found you.**
36   **HAGGAI: But I'm the one who found you!** *(Quickly)* **Never**

1   mind. Mouth is closed.

2   AMOS: *(To the SPOKESWOMAN)* **What do you think?**

3   SPOKESWOMAN: *(Places her hands on her hips and looks him over*

4   *from top to bottom.)* **Hmmmm. You've been hanging out**

5   **with the sinners again, haven't you?**

6   HAGGAI: *(Appalled)* **I'm not answering.**

7   SPOKESWOMAN: **That was not a question.** *(Continues to look*

8   *him over.)* **Looks like you've broken every single**

9   **commandment within the last forty-eight hours.**

10   HAGGAI: **Now, see here —**

11   SPOKESWOMAN: *(Holds up her hand.)* **Don't worry. I've seen**

12   **worse.**

13   AMOS: **Can you fix him?**

14   SPOKESWOMAN: *(Starts to chuckle.)* **Fix him? No. However, I**

15   **have just the thing.** *(She reaches under the table and pulls out*

16   *a paint can and brush and gives it to HAGGAI.)* **Here. Take this**

17   **behind the building and brush it all over your clothing.**

18   **Don't forget the back.**

19   AMOS: **Hurry before anyone sees you!** *(HAGGAI grabs the can*

20   *and brush and exits. AMOS faces the audience, pretending he*

21   *doesn't know the SPOKESWOMAN. SADDUCEE enters.)*

22   SADDUCEE: **Excuse me — are you the woman who helps the**

23   **Pharisees?**

24   SPOKESWOMAN: **I help all people who want to improve their**

25   **appearance.**

26   AMOS: **Get lost. No Sadducees allowed.**

27   SADDUCEE: **But I'm dirty!**

28   AMOS: *(Pushes him toward the exit.)* **Take a bath, and don't**

29   **bother us again.**

30   SADDUCEE: **But it doesn't help.**

31   AMOS: *(Calls Off-stage, toward HAGGAI.)* **Hurry up, Haggai! It's**

32   **getting crowded over here.**

33   HAGGAI: *(Enters dressed in a clean white robe with tassel. His face is*

34   *clean, and he's wearing a head covering. He hands the paint can*

35   *and brush to the SPOKESWOMAN.)* **Look at me. I'm pure**

36   **again!**

1   AMOS: Yeah, yeah, yeah. Let's go. We've got some sinners to
2   judge.
3   HAGGAI: Do we have to? They're so disgusting. *(HAGGAI and*
4   *AMOS exit.)*
5   SPOKESWOMAN: *(Holds up the can and addresses the audience.)*
6   Are you sad and tired of wearing the same dirty clothes
7   wrought with the decay of sin? Then try our Pharisee
8   Cleanser! It *whitewashes* over the filth to make you *look*
9   clean. After all, it's not who you are inside, but how clean
10   you appear to other people. So buy Pharisee Cleanser, and
11   perk up! There's no reason to be Sad-u-cee. *(Said like "sad,*
12   *you see.")*

Planting on the Highway

Theme
Evangelism, the Parable of the Sower

Scripture Reference
Ecclesiastes 11:4-6; Matthew 13:3-8; Mark 4:3-20;
Luke 8:11-15, John 3:16

Synopsis
A reporter relays the events of a deranged planter.

Cast
Holly
Leroy

Props
A microphone for the reporter.

Setting
Beside a highway

1   *(The reporter, HOLLY, is at Center Stage with LEROY standing*
2   *next to her.)*
3   HOLLY: Good evening. This is Holly Duran from the
4   _____ *(Insert your church or denomination)* news team.
5   I'm standing beside the interstate where a farmer was
6   seen planting seeds during the rush hour. *(Turns to*
7   *LEROY.)* Sir, could you tell us what you saw?
8   LEROY: Certainly. It started when I saw this guy in overalls
9   and a huge straw hat planting seeds in the park over
10   yonder. He started in the garden, but he was doing it all
11   wrong.
12   HOLLY: What do you mean?
13   LEROY: Well, he was just throwing them around. He never did
14   make any attempt to see that they were buried right. I'm a
15   farmer, you see, and I've planted seeds my whole life. I
16   can tell you from experience that he will lose most of his
17   seeds to birds if the wind doesn't blow them away first.
18   HOLLY: Since you are an experienced ... uh, seed planter
19   person, did you give this guy the benefit of your superior
20   knowledge?
21   LEROY: Of course. I just ... what?
22   HOLLY: Did you tell Overalls Man that he was doing it all
23   wrong?
24   LEROY: I even offered to help the clueless feller by showing
25   him how to space the seeds properly, how deep to bury
26   them, and how much to water them.
27   HOLLY: And what did the seed-thrower say?
28   LEROY: Nothing! He left and started spreading his seeds over
29   there among the rocks.
30   HOLLY: And what did you do then?
31   LEROY: I said, "Hold on there, dipstick — you're doing it all
32   wrong. Ain't no seed gonna grow among the rocks, and
33   the few that do manage to take root won't have much to
34   hold on to and will die from lack of water." Did he listen
35   to me? I think not, because the next thing he did was to
36   start planting on the highway!

1   HOLLY: So now he's in violation of littering.

2   LEROY: If he doesn't get himself killed first. A red Suburban

3   almost took him out, but he jumped over to the right lane

4   in the nick of time.

5   HOLLY: And what did you say to the highway scrambler?

6   LEROY: I said, "Hold on now, are you some kind of stupid?

7   You're gonna get run over trying to plant on concrete,"

8   and do you know what for?

9   HOLLY: No.

10   LEROY: Nothing! He's got a zillion to one shot at any seed

11   finding a crack to take root. But even if it did, it'd just get

12   squashed by a passing car.

13   HOLLY: So did the clueless wonder stop?

14   LEROY: Nope. We had to call the police to come and escort him

15   away.

16   HOLLY: Did he give any explanation for his erratic behavior?

17   LEROY: His what?

18   HOLLY: Did he give any statement as to why he was throwing

19   seeds around?

20   LEROY: Not really, but he did look at me with tears in his eyes

21   and said, "Just keep planting."

The Prayer Zone

Theme
Prayer, angels' protection

Scripture Reference
Psalm 103:20-22; Romans 8:37-39, 14:9

Synopsis
A man faces death unaware of what is happening.

Cast
Narrator (A Rod Serling type of character)
Larry Beckman
Grim Reaper
Angel

Costumes
Suit for the Narrator, Grim Reaper costume,
and angel costume

Props
Sickle for Grim Reaper and sword for Angel,
plus a sign saying "Bus Stop."

Setting
A bus stop. Hang up a sign saying "Bus Stop."

Note: *Twilight Zone*-type music adds to the spoof.

1   (*NARRATOR enters and addresses the audience.*)
2   **NARRATOR: There is a fifth dimension beyond that which is**
3   **known to man. It is a dimension as vast as space and as**
4   **timeless as infinity. It is the middle ground between light**
5   **and shadow, between science and superstition, and it lies**
6   **between the pit of man's fears and the summit of his**
7   **knowledge. This is the dimension of the spiritual. It is an**
8   **area that we call** *The Prayer Zone.* (*Music plays along the*
9   *lines of* The Twilight Zone's *theme song.*)
10 **The place is here. The time is now. And the journey**
11 **into the prayer life that we're about to watch could be our**
12 **own journey.** (*LARRY enters. He walks up to the bus stop sign.*)
13 **Street scene. Summer. The present. The man next to the**
14 **bus stop is Larry Beckman, age fortyish. Occupation:**
15 **salesman. In just a few moments, Larry will have to**
16 **concern himself with survival, because as of five o'clock**
17 **this mild September day, he'll be stalked by Mr. Death.**
18 (*More* Twilight Zone-*type music plays. GRIM REAPER enters.*
19 *He spots LARRY and approaches him, raising his sickle. ANGEL*
20 *enters. He raises his sword and blocks the GRIM REAPER from*
21 *reaching LARRY. They battle, sword against sickle. LARRY is*
22 *oblivious to the fight behind him. He checks his watch, then chews*
23 *on his fingernails.*)
24 **What Larry doesn't know is that at this very minute, his**
25 **grandmother is praying for him. She's prayed for him his**
26 **entire life, but tonight she's praying extra hard. Why, you**
27 **ask? Let's just say she's got connections with those of the**
28 **unseen.** (*The ANGEL defeats the GRIM REAPER and chases*
29 *him away.*)
30 **Larry Beckman, age fortyish. Occupation: salesman.**
31 **Throughout his life, he seemed to beat death's back door.**
32 **Couldn't happen, you say? Probably not in most places,**
33 **but it did happen in The Prayer Zone.** (*More* Twilight Zone
34 -*type music as the CAST exits.*)

The Prayer Zone 2

Theme
Prayer

Scripture Reference
Ephesians 6:12

Synopsis
A woman sees a gremlin that no one else sees.
Is it a hallucination or divine intervention?

Cast
Narrator
Edwina
Passenger
Captain's Voice (Off-stage)
Several extras

Costumes
A suit for the Narrator

Props
Backpack for parachute

Setting
An airplane. Line up four or more chairs with
a center aisle to simulate an aircraft.

Note: *Twilight Zone*-type music adds to the spoof.

1 NARRATOR: *(Enters and faces the audience.)* **There is a fifth**
2 **dimension beyond that which is known to man. It is a**
3 **dimension as vast as space and as timeless as infinity. It is**
4 **the middle ground between light and darkness, between**
5 **heaven and hell, and it lies between the pit of man's fears**
6 **and the summit of his knowledge. This is the dimension**
7 **of the spiritual. It is an area we call "The Prayer Zone."**
8 *(Music similar to* The Twilight Zone *TV show plays. EDWINA*
9 *FRUMKIST enters. She walks down an aisle of chairs and takes*
10 *her place in the first row.)* **Portrait of a frightened woman.**
11 **Mrs. Edwina Frumkist, age thirty-two. Wife and mother**
12 **who has just been released from the hospital where she**
13 **spent the last two months recovering from a nervous**
14 **breakdown. Today she is traveling by air all the way to**
15 **her chosen destination, which — contrary to the world of**
16 **sanity — happens to be the deepest corner of The Prayer**
17 **Zone.** *(More* Twilight Zone-*type music.)*
18 EDWINA: Uh-oh — there's something outside the window!
19 PASSENGER: *(Dryly)* Yeah, they're called clouds.
20 EDWINA: No! It's a little gremlin trying to destroy the airplane!
21 PASSENGER: Oh, brother — and I bet it's chewing on the
22   wires.
23 EDWINA: No, he's using a chainsaw.
24 PASSENGER: Of all the days to be sitting next to a loony tune.
25 EDWINA: We've got to do something. Does anyone have a
26   gun?
27 PASSENGER: Are you crazy, lady? No one is allowed to bring
28   guns on a plane. Chill out, will ya?
29 EDWINA: Are you telling me that you don't see the little green
30   gremlin?
31 PASSENGER: That's exactly what I'm telling you. We're not in
32   any danger here.
33 EDWINA: But we are! We need a parachute. Doesn't this plane
34   have any protection against green monster creatures?
35   *(EXTRA hands a parachute to EDWINA, who slips it on.)*
36 PASSENGER: *(Sighs.)* Holy mother of —

1 EDWINA: God! We need to pray to God. Let's all get down on
2 our knees.
3 PASSENGER: Are you insane?
4 EDWINA: *(Drops to her knees.)* Heavenly Father, protect us from
5 that green goblin person.
6 PASSENGER: Leave me out of this. I want no part of your God.
7 EDWINA: OK, then — protect *me*, dear Lord, from that green
8 goblin person.
9 PASSENGER: You're wasting your breath.
10 CAPTAIN'S VOICE: *(From Off-stage)* Attention, all passengers.
11 We have just lost power to our main engine. We're
12 descending rapidly. Please stand by. *(All PASSENGERS*
13 *scream and take the crash position, with their hands covering*
14 *their bent heads. EDWINA gets up, puts on the backpack, and*
15 *jumps out. Blackout. Everyone exits except the NARRATOR.)*
16 NARRATOR: Edwina Frumkist, sole survivor of flight 254.
17 Found alive and well, floating among the wreckage of
18 that doomed flight. Was it a hallucination or a spiritual
19 awakening that saved her that day? Mrs. Edwina
20 Frumkist, heading home after taking an important detour
21 through The Prayer Zone.

Quest for Fire

Theme
Holy Spirit, Pentecost

Scripture Reference
Acts 2:4

Synopsis
Two Neanderthal men find spiritual enlightenment.

Cast
Neanderthal 1
Neanderthal 2
Woman
Man

Costumes
Crude robes for Neanderthal 1 and 2, tie for Man

Props
Two sticks, a large cross, Bible, purse loaded with keys
and odd items (use your imagination), lighter

Setting
Outside

Director's Notes: This is a fun sketch with lots of grunting, groans, and exaggerated gestures. Overacting highly encouraged.

1   *(NEANDERTHAL 1 and 2 enter grunting and pointing at various*
2   *objects around the stage. NEANDERTHAL 1 carries two sticks*
3   *and starts rubbing them together while NEANDERTHAL 2*
4   *gestures that he should hurry the process. NEANDERTHAL 2*
5   *finally loses patience and grabs the sticks away from*
6   *NEANDERTHAL 1 and continues to rub the sticks together.*
7   *NEANDERTHAL 1 grunts his discontent, then looks around the*
8   *room. He grabs a large cross, very pleased with his prize.*
9   *NEANDERTHAL 2, points and grunts loudly at*
10   *NEANDERTHAL 1, who very gently places the cross back where*
11   *he found it.*
12   *NEANDERTHAL 2 then finds a Bible. He jumps up and*
13   *down in excitement, pointing and showing the audience what he*
14   *has. He then hugs and rocks the Bible. NEANDERTHAL 1*
15   *gestures for him to come over to him. NEANDERTHAL 2 shakes*
16   *his head and holds the Bible tighter. NEANDERTHAL 1 grunts*
17   *his discontent and gestures with both arms. NEANDERTHAL 2*
18   *shakes his head. NEANDERTHAL 1 drops his sticks in*
19   *frustration, then looks around at the audience. He hobbles over to*
20   *a WOMAN and begins to check inside her purse. He finds keys*
21   *and jingles them together like a toy. NEANDERTHAL 2, still*
22   *clutching his Bible, points and tries to get NEANDERTHAL 1 to*
23   *bring the keys over. NEANDERTHAL 1 grunts, shakes his head,*
24   *then reconsiders and tosses the keys to NEANDERTHAL 2, who*
25   *shakes them a bit, then quickly loses interest and tosses them on*
26   *the floor. Meanwhile, NEANDERTHAL 1 continues to search*
27   *the WOMAN's purse, pulling out several articles that don't*
28   *necessarily belong in a purse. He becomes frustrated and empties*
29   *the entire contents on the floor. He then looks over at a MAN*
30   *sitting in the aisle and starts to reach for his tie. The MAN pulls*
31   *out a lighter and flicks it.)*
32   **MAN: Back. Get back!**
33   **NEANDERTHAL 1:** *(In awe)* **Ohhhh!** *(NEANDERTHAL 1 grabs*
34   *the lighter and jumps around with excitement, showing the*
35   *audience what he has. NEANDERTHAL 2 grunts and gestures*
36   *for NEANDERTHAL 1 to come back to the stage.*

1   *NEANDERTHAL 1 hobbles back and shows NEANDERTHAL 2*
2   *the lighter. He then flicks the lighter and holds it above the head of*
3   *NEANDERTHAL 2, who immediately straightens up and opens*
4   *the Bible.)*
5   **NEANDERTHAL 2:** *(Reading)* **And suddenly there came a**
6   **sound from heaven as of a rushing, mighty wind, and it**
7   **filled the house where they were all sitting.**
8   **NEANDERTHAL 1: Ooooh?** *(Looks amazed at audience, then flicks*
9   *the lighter over his head and immediately straightens his stance as*
10   *NEANDERTHAL 2 continues reading.)*
11   **NEANDERTHAL 2: And they were filled with the Holy Ghost**
12   **and began to speak with other tongues.**
13   **NEANDERTHAL 1: Whoa! Imagine speaking another**
14   **language. It was like they suddenly became smart!**
15   **NEANDERTHAL 2: Oh, I think it's more than that. I think**
16   **being filled with the Spirit gives you that *connection* with**
17   **the Father.**
18   **NEANDERTHAL 1:** *(Nods in agreement.)* **That spiritual oneness**
19   **in discerning the will of God.**
20   **NEANDERTHAL 2: Exactly.** *(They start to exit.)* **What are those**
21   **sticks doing there?**
22   **NEANDERTHAL 1: I have no idea.**

Rescue Me

Theme
Listening to God

Scripture Reference
Psalm 30:1

Synopsis
A person has great faith, but deaf ears.

Cast
Troy
Kim
Bill
Dee
Sandee
St. Peter

Props
Oars optional. Boat, raft, and helicopter are pantomimed.

Setting
Outside, in a flood. Chairs may be stacked to provide
an image of standing on a roof.

1 (TROY, KIM, BILL, DEE, and SANDEE stand at Center Stage
2 looking panicked.)
3 **KIM:** The flood waters are coming in!
4 **BILL:** Oh, no! Quick — everyone go to higher ground.
5 **KIM:** Where do we go?
6 **TROY:** My roof. Hurry — everyone climb on. (ALL climb on the
7 chairs.)
8 **KIM:** This is horrible. When will this storm end?
9 **BILL:** The waters keep rising.
10 **TROY:** Fear not. My God will save us.
11 **KIM:** Do you really believe that?
12 **BILL:** I never trusted in God too much before.
13 **TROY:** All we have to do is pray for a miracle.
14 **KIM:** Oh, great. We're doomed.
15 **BILL:** You mean pray for God to rescue us?
16 **TROY:** Rescue? O ye of little faith. We're going to pray for a
17   miracle! A bonafide, parting-of-the-Red-Sea miracle.
18   (Raises arms.) O Lord, grant us a miracle to save us. Wash
19   away these waters so that we can walk out of here on dry
20   land. (DEE enters, pantomiming paddling a boat.)
21 **DEE:** Hey, I've got a canoe. I can take one of you with me.
22 **TROY:** Can't you see I'm praying here? We're praying for all of
23   us to be saved, not just one.
24 **KIM:** You go ahead and pray. I'm leaving. (She hops into the canoe
25   and the two of them paddle away.)
26 **TROY:** (Calls after them.) You're going to miss the big event!
27   (Back to praying) As King David said, "You are my rescue."
28   We are trusting for you to intercede and rescue us, just as
29   you did with David.
30 **BILL:** Hey, look — it's a raft. Come on, let's jump on it and get
31   to safety.
32 **TROY:** That's just an old piece of wood. You could flip over and
33   drown. Stay and see what God is going to do. You'll see a
34   real miracle.
35 **BILL:** But the waters are almost to the roof!
36 **TROY:** God often answers miracles at the eleventh hour. I'll

1   keep praying, and you'll see.

2   BILL: I'm taking the raft. *(BILL jumps down and uses both arms to*

3   *paddle away.)*

4   TROY: Your loss! *(Back to praying)* **Forgive those of little faith,**

5   **Lord. Just as it takes faith the size of a mustard seed to**

6   **move mountains, I believe you can move these waters so**

7   **I can climb down on dry land.**

8   SANDEE: *(Enters pantomiming flying a helicopter.)* **Hey down**

9   **there, we'll drop you a rope. Climb up the ladder to our**

10   **helicopter, and we'll take you to safety.**

11   TROY: **Back off! I'm praying for a miracle here. I'm going to**

12   **walk away from these floodwaters.**

13   SANDEE: **Mister, no one is going to walk away. Take the rope.**

14   TROY: *(Dismissive wave)* **Go rescue someone who has less faith**

15   **than I do. There's a guy floating on a raft somewhere**

16   **around here.** *(SANDEE flies away. TROY steps down from the*

17   *roof and walks over to the far side of the stage. ST. PETER comes*

18   *out to meet him.)*

19   TROY: **Where am I?**

20   ST. PETER: **You're in heaven.**

21   TROY: **Heaven? You mean I died?**

22   ST. PETER: **It sure looks that way.**

23   TROY: **But — but I prayed for a miracle. Why didn't God save**

24   **me?**

25   ST. PETER: **He sent you a boat, a raft, and a helicopter. What**

26   **more did you want?**

27   TROY: **I wanted to walk away on dry land.**

28   ST. PETER: **Dude, when God sends help, just get in the boat.**

Saga of Free Will

Theme
Obedience

Scripture Reference
1 Samuel 15:1-9; Esther 3:1

Synopsis
King Saul thinks he knows better than God,
but his decision threatens the future.

Cast
Michael
Gabriel
Lieutenant
Saul
Messenger
Deborah

Costumes
Angel robes (or choir robes) for Michael and Gabriel
and biblical robes for the rest.

Props
A large scroll, a large book, and a pen and pad of paper, table

Setting
Heaven and a biblical battlefield

1   *(GABRIEL sits on the edge of the table. MICHAEL enters and*
2   *hands GABRIEL a scroll.)*
3   **MICHAEL:** Gabriel, I have an important message for you to
4   deliver to the prophet Samuel.
5   **GABRIEL:** Wow, it's marked "urgent." It must be about the war
6   with the Israelites and the Amalekites.
7   **MICHAEL:** Make sure Samuel gives it to Saul. The future of
8   the Israelites is dependent on him following these
9   instructions to the letter.
10   **GABRIEL:** To the letter. I got it. *(As GABRIEL starts to exit, he*
11   *opens the scroll and peeks inside. MICHAEL exits.*
12   *LIEUTENANT and SAUL enter.)*
13   **LIEUTENANT:** Our armies have overtaken the Amalekites, my
14   King. What are your orders?
15   **SAUL:** Gather all the spoils and divide among the troops.
16   **MESSENGER:** *(Runs up to SAUL.)* King Saul ... Saul, I have a
17   message from the prophet Samuel.
18   **SAUL:** Wait a minute, Lieutenant. I'm sure Samuel has a
19   message from God about the victory at hand.
20   **MESSENGER:** Yes, my King. He said to destroy everything.
21   **SAUL:** Everything?
22   **MESSENGER:** Everything. He said to kill the soldiers, men,
23   women, children, oxen, cattle, dogs, cats, chickens, gold,
24   silver —
25   **LIEUTENANT:** *(Interrupting)* I think we get the picture.
26   **SAUL:** Wow. What about King Agag?
27   **MESSENGER:** Kill him.
28   **SAUL:** The women and children?
29   **MESSENGER:** Kill them.
30   **SAUL:** Surely he meant only the ugly women.
31   **MESSENGER:** All of them.
32   **SAUL:** What about the gold?
33   **MESSENGER:** Destroy it.
34   **LIEUTENANT:** *(To SAUL)* What should I do to one who brings
35   such bad news?
36   **MESSENGER:** *(Holds his hands up.)* Hey, don't kill the

1   messenger.

2   SAUL: What should I do? It all seems so cruel!

3   LIEUTENANT: Perhaps the messenger misunderstood the
4   prophet.

5   MESSENGER: I beg your pardon. I am a professional.

6   SAUL: It would be such a waste to destroy them.

7   LIEUTENANT: I agree, Your Majesty. Perhaps we could spare
8   the cattle?

9   SAUL: Yes, yes, our troops need food. We'll just kill the sick
10   ones.

11   LIEUTENANT: *(Writing down on a pad of paper.)* Sick ones. Got it.

12   SAUL: And their army. Kill anyone in uniform.

13   LIEUTENANT: The women too?

14   SAUL: Are you nuts?

15   LIEUTENANT: What about King Agag?

16   SAUL: *(Thinks for a moment.)* Spare the King and all that is good
17   within his court.

18   MESSENGER: What's considered good?

19   LIEUTENANT: The women.

20   SAUL: I like women.

21   MESSENGER: Shouldn't we do everything the Lord instructs?
22   After all, he's always looked out for our best interests.

23   SAUL: Hey, we're doing *most* of what he wants. You can't
24   expect us to be unreasonable about demands that don't
25   make sense.

26   LIEUTENANT: Are you talking about the destruction of gold?

27   SAUL: I'm talking about the women!

28   LIEUTENANT: The pretty ones.

29   SAUL: Now you understand.

30   LIEUTENANT: It shall be done, my King. *(ALL exit. GABRIEL*
31   *and MICHAEL enter.)*

32   MICHAEL: No, no, no. Has he lost his mind?

33   GABRIEL: I delivered the message as instructed, but Saul
34   chose not to follow it.

35   MICHAEL: You see, this is the problem I have with free will. I
36   knew it was a bad idea from the beginning. I told the

1   Lord, I said, "Don't put that fruit tree in the Garden of
2   Eden. You know someone will eventually eat it." Did he
3   listen to me? I think not!
4   GABRIEL: Why is it so important to eliminate this race?
5   MICHAEL: Their survival means the destruction of millions of
6   Jews in the future. The Lord has seen this.
7   GABRIEL: And Saul didn't do as he was told?
8   MICHAEL: No.
9   GABRIEL: So now the future of the Jews is in danger?
10   MICHAEL: From the seed that was spared, a man will be born
11   whose only goal in life is to kill every last Jew on the face
12   of the planet.
13   GABRIEL: Hitler?
14   MICHAEL: No. Haman the Agagite.
15   GABRIEL: Ah, I get it. King Agag's descendants.
16   MICHAEL: Exactly.
17   GABRIEL: So what will the Lord do now?
18   MICHAEL: There's always a plan, Gabriel. *(DEBORAH enters*
19   *and hands MICHAEL a very large book. MICHAEL plunks it on*
20   *the table.)* We now have to add the book of Esther.
21   GABRIEL: That's a large book!
22   MICHAEL: Oh, this is her entire life. The significant parts will
23   be edited down for public viewing.
24   GABRIEL: So she singlehandedly saves the Jewish nation?
25   MICHAEL: That's right.
26   DEBORAH: Ironic, don't you think?
27   MICHAEL: What?
28   DEBORAH: Man messes up, and it takes a woman to save the
29   day.

Sharing the Peace

Theme
Peace vs. contention

Scripture Reference
Romans 14:9

Synopsis
A husband and wife discuss a not-so-peaceful, soon-to-be-disastrous scenario.

Cast
Husband
Wife

Props
None

Setting
The lobby of a church

Note: Keep the conversation light, as though the husband and wife are discussing an upcoming fun event. No anger should be detected in the conversation.

1 *(The scene begins with the HUSBAND and WIFE standing at*
2 *Center Stage greeting the congregation.)*
3 WIFE: Wasn't the church service wonderful?!
4 HUSBAND: "Living your life through Christ." Always a good
5   sermon topic.
6 WIFE: I especially liked the singing.
7 HUSBAND: The choir did a great job harmonizing.
8 WIFE: They brought a tear to my eye.
9 HUSBAND: I'm glad we come here every Sunday.
10 WIFE: Me too. Isn't it nice how we can agree on spending time
11   in worship?
12 HUSBAND: It's easy when you're surrounded by spirit-filled
13   people. The love of God flows through the pews.
14 WIFE: When we're worshiping the Lord, all of the petty things
15   we disagree on seem so insignificant.
16 HUSBAND: You're right.
17 WIFE: Like the art gallery we're going to this afternoon.
18 HUSBAND: Oh, yeah. As always, you'll pick out some
19   painting that looks like a preschooler gone wild ...
20 WIFE: While you insist on stupid still-life photos.
21 HUSBAND: Oh, we are going to have such a fight!
22 WIFE: I am going to be so mad at you ...
23 HUSBAND: Incidents from past arguments will spew from
24   your mouth ...
25 WIFE: And I'm sure I'll find a way to blame your mother.
26 HUSBAND: The name calling ...
27 WIFE: The crying and screaming ...
28 HUSBAND: It's going to get ugly.
29 WIFE: But not now.
30 HUSBAND: Nope, not now. *(Turns to a member of the*
31   *congregation.)* **Good morning, _____.** *(Insert member's*
32   *name.)* **God's blessings to you.**
33 WIFE: **Hi, _____.** *(Insert member's name.)* **Peace to you and**
34   **your family.** *(They both exit, smiling and sharing the peace with*
35   *the congregation.)*

Show Us the Love

Theme
Love

Scripture Reference
1 Corinthians 13:4-7; Philippians 2:1-2; 1 Peter 2:17

Synopsis
Two athletes have entirely different views
on the definition of love.

Cast
Suzie – The soccer player
Bruce – The football player

Costumes
Appropriate jerseys for each player

Props
A soccer ball and a football for the athletes to carry

1   *(SUZIE and BRUCE enter from opposite sides of the stage and*
2   *introduce themselves.)*
3   SUZIE: Hi! I'm Suzie, and I play soccer.
4   BRUCE: I'm Bruce, and I play football.
5   SUZIE: Soccer requires a lot of skill.
6   BRUCE: Football requires a lot of hitting.
7   SUZIE: In soccer, we work together as a team to get the ball in
8   the goal.
9   BRUCE: In football, we annihilate the little guys to get the ball
10   across the goal.
11   SUZIE: Our sport requires everyone working in unison down
12   the field.
13   BRUCE: Our sport requires brute force and hitting at the same
14   time!
15   SUZIE; When we're angry with each other, we usually gather in
16   a circle, hold hands, and talk about our problems.
17   BRUCE: When we're angry with each other, we just tape the
18   little guy to the goalpost and call it good.
19   SUZIE: We show love by jumping up and down and hugging
20   each other.
21   BRUCE: We show love by slapping the guy across the helmet a
22   few times. But if we're really happy, we'll pour ice-cold
23   Gatorade down his back.
24   SUZIE: We show compassion by listening to the needs of each
25   other.
26   BRUCE: Hey, whenever our guys are feeling down, we give the
27   little guy a wedgie, and it perks everyone right up.
28   SUZIE: Except for the "little guy."
29   BRUCE: Hey, the "little guy" knows his place among the love.
30   SUZIE: Love? Slapping people around, pouring ice down their
31   backs, taping people to goal posts, you call that love?
32   BRUCE: It's all in the translation.
33   SUZIE: I'll never understand guys.

Snakes Are So Misunderstood

Theme
Spiritual warfare, Satan

Scripture Reference
Genesis 3:1-15; 1 Peter 5:8

Synopsis
The Serpent's influence is everywhere, and it's poison.

Cast
Satan

Costumes
A devil costume with a toy snake worn around the neck

Props
None

Setting
Nonspecific

1   (*SATAN enters and addresses the audience.*)
2   SATAN: Ah, good, you're all here. Now don't panic. Just
3   because I'm here doesn't mean you're down *there* — so to
4   speak. Actually, I'm here because of the gross
5   misrepresentation of my friend, the snake. Isn't he
6   beautiful? Yet, this poor pitiful creature was struck down
7   five thousand years ago and denied his rightful place
8   among the animal kingdom.
9   Once upon a time — I've always wanted to say that —
10   once upon a time, this beautiful creature had legs. Lots of
11   them. But unlike the lowly centipede, this creature
12   walked wherever his legs would take him. He loved the
13   trees, for he had digits to grasp the branches. He could
14   hide on the highest limb and hear the conversations of the
15   two humans below. Oh, they were clueless, those two —
16   simpletons, actually. It didn't even dawn on the woman
17   that anything was out of the ordinary when I started
18   talking to her — I mean, when *it* started talking. Before
19   you could say "fig leaf," those two were cast out of the
20   greatest garden ever created.
21   However, in an unfair turn of events, I was ... I mean,
22   *he* was stripped of his legs and forced to crawl on his
23   belly forever! Do you know how degrading that is? From
24   that moment on, he's had to slither from place to place,
25   spreading his poison on any unsuspecting victim who
26   dared cross his path. Cruel, you say? Why shouldn't he
27   get revenge for what the Almighty did to him? Cleopatra
28   fell to the serpent's bite. It was too easy. But the apostle
29   Paul didn't have the decency to drop dead even after I ...
30   *it* hung on for a long time! Can you imagine how
31   annoying that is? And to spite all my — er, *his* efforts,
32   Christianity continues to grow.
33   Don't let his humbling appearance deceive you. He's
34   resorted to other methods to make you come to your
35   senses, and they can be found in your church. Shocked,
36   are you? "It could never happen to us," you say. Ha! I've

1   been planting snakes for centuries. My favorite is the
2   slow poison kind. You know, those that constantly
3   complain about how the church is run, and they can never
4   see any good. Yeah, I love that type. They can wear down
5   a church in no time and strip it of its joy. I hate happy
6   people.
7   My second favorite snake is in your mind. Didn't know
8   you had creepy crawling creatures squeezing your head,
9   now did you? Yes, this snake is very effective. Once he has
10 a hold on you, he'll make you feel like you're all alone
11 and helpless. It won't even occur to the clueless wonder to
12 call out to the guy upstairs. It just squeezes and chokes
13 until any sense of higher power is gone and the victim
14 thinks he has to make it on his own. Oh, don't worry —
15 when he reaches that point, I send other snakes to keep
16 him company. After all, the snake is a friendly, social
17 creature. Ever see a den full of snakes all cuddled together
18 in a wiggly mass? Yes, keep that image in mind. It could
19 end up being inside you. But then, that wouldn't be so
20 bad, *(Turns to snake and talks to it)* would it, Pookie? Yes,
21 you're such a disgusting, slithery thing. Give Daddy some
22 love. *(Kisses the snake.)*
23   Now if you'll excuse us, we're heading out to brunch.
24 Pookie loves to feed on all the unhappy Christians as they
25 complain about their church, the pastor, and anyone else
26 in the congregation. They're great recruiters for my side.
27 *(Exits.)*

That's Not in the Script

Theme
Obedience

Scripture Reference
Deuteronomy 1, 4:32-38; Numbers 13

Synopsis
The Headmaster angel is flabbergasted when the Israelites want to deviate from God's plan.

Cast
Headmaster
Angel
Messenger

Costumes
Angel robes for all (or choir robes work just as well)

Props
The Bible with an extra page to simulate ripping it out, or a stack of papers to represent a manuscript

Setting
Heaven

1   *(ANGEL rushes in to the HEADMASTER angel who is looking*
2   *over the script/Bible.)*
3   ANGEL: Headmaster, there's some important information from
4   earth.
5   HEADMASTER: Ah, there you are. We've got a lot of work to
6   do. You said you just came from earth?
7   ANGEL: Yes sir, but there's been an incident ...
8   HEADMASTER: Moses *did* rescue the people from Egypt, did
9   he not?
10   ANGEL: Oh, yes indeed, sir. In fact, they're in the desert right
11   now.
12   HEADMASTER: Then there's nothing to worry about. All is
13   going according to plan, just as God ordained it.
14   ANGEL: Yes, but there's been a slight setback.
15   HEADMASTER: Setback? The Israelites didn't drop the Ten
16   Commandments, did they?
17   ANGEL: Well, no, but —
18   HEADMASTER: It's a good thing. Those tablets are not made
19   of clay, you know.
20   ANGEL: I know.
21   HEADMASTER: They have to be taken care of.
22   ANGEL: I'm proud to say they're following the Lord's
23   instructions to the letter.
24   HEADMASTER: No deviations?
25   ANGEL: None.
26   HEADMASTER: Every "i" dotted?
27   ANGEL: Every "t" crossed.
28   HEADMASTER: So what seems to be the problem?
29   ANGEL: Well, you know the Israelites are camped in the desert
30   of Paran.
31   HEADMASTER: Ah, yes, they're getting ready to enter Canaan,
32   the hill country of the Amorites.
33   ANGEL: Yes, sir.
34   HEADMASTER: *(Chuckles.)* Those heathens don't have a clue
35   what's coming, do they?
36   ANGEL: Well ...

1 HEADMASTER: With God before Israel's army, who can stop
2   them? Don't you agree?
3 ANGEL: You would think so.
4 HEADMASTER: All that's left now is to simply waltz in and
5   take the land. The entire territory has heard what God did
6   to the Egyptians, and they are scared to death. So what
7   seems to be the problem?
8 ANGEL: They won't go.
9 HEADMASTER: What? What are you talking about?
10 ANGEL: They refuse to go into the Promised Land.
11 HEADMASTER: That's preposterous. That's not in the script!
12   *(Holds up Bible/manuscript.)* It says right here that the Lord
13   created a fear in the hearts of the Canaanites who fled
14   their homes, leaving the land to the Israelites without so
15   much as raising a sword.
16 ANGEL: Are you sure that's what it says?
17 HEADMASTER: I just read it to you, didn't I? *(MESSENGER*
18   *enters.)*
19 MESSENGER: Excuse me, sir. *(Takes the manuscript and rips a*
20   *page out, then hands the manuscript back to the HEADMASTER*
21   *and exits.)*
22 HEADMASTER: I don't understand what went wrong.
23 ANGEL: The Israelites sent in twelve spies to scope the land
24   and see what they're up against.
25 HEADMASTER: A prudent move for those about to conquer a
26   land, but unnecessary for the Israelites, since the Lord
27   said he was giving it to them.
28 ANGEL: They came back with glowing reports about a land of
29   milk and honey.
30 HEADMASTER: Naturally.
31 ANGEL: And then they convinced everyone else not to go in.
32 HEADMASTER: All of them?
33 ANGEL: Except for Caleb and Joshua. They tried to rally the
34   crowd with the old "win one for the Gipper" speech, but
35   no one would bite.
36 HEADMASTER: You mean after all the Lord has done, they

1   still don't believe?

2   ANGEL: No sir.

3   HEADMASTER: But — but he led them with a cloud of fire!

4   ANGEL: I know.

5   HEADMASTER: He parted the Red Sea!

6   ANGEL: Split it right in two. Killed Pharaoh and his army.

7   HEADMASTER: He fed them manna and gave them water out
8   of a rock!

9   ANGEL: Tastiest water in all of Egypt.

10   HEADMASTER: And they don't believe him?

11   ANGEL: Nope.

12   HEADMASTER: That's the most idiotic thing I've ever heard
13   of.

14   ANGEL: Hey, you're preaching to the choir.

15   HEADMASTER: Who gave them the authority to change the
16   script?

17   ANGEL: The Lord did.

18   HEADMASTER: What? How?

19   ANGEL: It's called "free will."

20   HEADMASTER: So what you're telling me is that they have the
21   option to mess up God's perfect plan for their life. What's
22   going to happen now? *(MESSENGER enters.)*

23   MESSENGER: *(Hands him a ream of paper.)* Here you go, sir. New
24   plans.

25   ANGEL: The Lord always has a plan, even though the humans
26   mess it up.

27   HEADMASTER: Forty years? It's going to take that long to get
28   to the Promised Land?

29   ANGEL: It seems ironic, don't you think? They're still going to
30   get there, but they've chosen the long way.

31   HEADMASTER: Not to mention an awful waste of paper.

Thunderclouds and Lightning Bolts

Theme
Listening, God's voice

Scripture Reference
Matthew 13:13-15

Synopsis
A prospective student's choice of college seems
clear until she turns a deaf ear to the call.

Cast
Chloe
Beth
Kristin
Lauren

Props
Papers

Setting
At home. Place a couple chairs at Center Stage,
as well as a table if you wish.

1   (*BETH sits at Center Stage, rifling through papers.*)
2   CHLOE: Hi, Beth. What are you doing?
3   BETH: I'm trying to decide which college to go to. I've been
4   accepted into a prestigious out-of-state school, but I've
5   also been accepted to this state school.
6   CHLOE: That seems easy enough. Go to the prestigious one.
7   BETH: But it's so expensive! Besides, I can get just as good of a
8   degree with the state college. I guess I'll just have to pray
9   about it some more.
10   CHLOE: You're lucky you *have* a choice of colleges. I didn't get
11   accepted at the one I wanted to go to. I keep asking God
12   for direction, but I still don't know where to go.
13   BETH: You only applied to one college? Have you tried any
14   others?
15   CHLOE: Why should I? There was only one I wanted.
16   BETH: But sometimes what we want isn't the best choice for us.
17   God often closes one door before he opens another door.
18   CHLOE: Well, I did get accepted into a tech college, but that's
19   not what I want. Besides, they'll accept anyone at those
20   schools, so how in the world do I know it's God's
21   direction? (*KRISTIN enters with papers.*)
22   KRISTIN: Chloe, Mom told me to give you these papers.
23   CHLOE: What is it?
24   KRISTIN: You've qualified for a full grant at the tech school.
25   BETH: That's wonderful! This is the answer you're looking for.
26   CHLOE: Oh, big deal. They're always looking for someone to
27   give their grants to. It's just a crummy tech school.
28   Besides, I doubt I would be able to work school around
29   my job. (*LAUREN enters.*)
30   LAUREN: Chloe, your boss called, and he approved your
31   request to work strictly on the weekends.
32   BETH: Wow! It all worked out like it was meant to be.
33   CHLOE: I just wish I knew if this was God's direction for my
34   life.
35   BETH: I don't understand.
36   CHLOE: I don't hear his voice. I need clear direction on what to

1   do next.
2   BETH: Are you kidding me? He's screaming at you, but you're
3   not listening.
4   CHLOE: No, I think you're wrong, and I'm not accepting any
5   scholarship or grant until I know for sure.
6   BETH: Chloe, if you can't hear God in the whispers of every
7   day, you're not going to hear him in thunderclouds and
8   lightning bolts. *(Pause)* Chloe, are you listening to me?
9   CHLOE: Hmmmm? Look, I'm gonna go someplace quiet where
10   I can hear the voice of the Lord touching my heart. There's
11   too much racket around here. Maybe I should forget
12   school altogether. Minimum wage isn't so bad once you
13   get used to it. *(CHLOE exits.)*
14   KRISTIN: What do you make of that?
15   LAUREN: I think that while Chloe is trying to figure out if God
16   is speaking to her, she's going to end up repeating those
17   seven little words.
18   KRISTIN: What seven little words?
19   LAUREN: "Would you like fries with that, sir?"

The Trial of Job

Theme
Contentment, faithfulness

Scripture Reference
Job (entire book)

Synopsis
Job is tested for his faith.

Cast

God	Satan
Job	Narrator
Servant 1	Servant 2
Servant 3	Servant 4
Eliphaz	Bildad
Zophar	

Note: For smaller groups, the Servants, friends, and Narrator may be doubled. This sketch was originally performed by young players from 8-10 years old.

Costumes
Biblical robes for most of cast, plus a white robe for God and a red cape or other red clothing for Satan.

Props
Bucket of water or confetti, depending on your performing venue

Setting
Job's home in the biblical land of Uz.

1   *(NARRATOR is in place behind the podium.)*

2   NARRATOR: This is the story of Job and how he remained

3   faithful to God, even when his whole life was crumbling

4   around him. *(GOD and SATAN enter from opposite sides of the*

5   *stage.)*

6   SATAN: Hello, God.

7   GOD: Satan, what are you doing here?

8   SATAN: Oh, I'm just hanging out, watching my favorite

9   program, *The Fall of Mankind*. It's most entertaining.

10   GOD: Have you noticed my servant Job? He honors me and

11   stays away from evil.

12   SATAN: *(Sarcastic, hands on hips)* Well, yeah! It's easy to be

13   faithful when you've made him the richest man in the

14   area. But I bet if you were to take that all away, he'd turn

15   on you in a heartbeat.

16   GOD: You have my permission to do as you will, but under no

17   circumstances are you to harm him.

18   SATAN: I'll take that bet. *(SATAN and GOD exit. JOB enters.*

19   *SERVANT 1 enters shortly after.)*

20   SERVANT 1: Job, thieves came and stole all your oxen and

21   donkeys. I alone escaped to tell you.

22   JOB: Oh no, that's terrible news. But I still love God. *(SERVANT*

23   *1 steps Upstage. GOD runs across stage, arms raised in victory,*

24   *then exits. SATAN runs after him, pulling at his hair and clearly*

25   *agitated, and exits also. SERVANT 2 enters.)*

26   SERVANT 2: Hi, Job.

27   JOB: Hi, servant.

28   SERVANT 2: Um … how's it going?

29   JOB: I just got some terrible news. My donkeys and oxen have

30   been stolen.

31   SERVANT 2: Well, I have a bit of terrible news, too.

32   JOB: What happened?

33   SERVANT 2: It was the weirdest thing. Lightning fell from the

34   sky and burned up all your sheep and servants. Luckily, I

35   escaped to tell you.

36   JOB: Well, I'm glad you're safe, but all my poor sheep … I still

1 **love God, though.** *(SERVANT 2 steps Upstage. GOD runs*
2 *across stage in victory, then exits. SATAN follows, shaking his*
3 *head. SERVANT 3 enters.)*
4 **SERVANT 3: Job, the Babylonians attacked and took all your**
5 **camels.**
6 **JOB: Not my camels!**
7 **SERVANT 3: They killed all your servants, too.**
8 **JOB: Not my servants!**
9 **SERVANT 3: I'm still alive.**
10 **JOB: Thank the Lord for that. Wow, this is the worst day of my**
11 **life. But I still love God.** *(SERVANT 3 steps Upstage. GOD*
12 *runs across the stage in victory, then exits. SATAN follows,*
13 *looking frustrated. SERVANT 4 enters.)*
14 **SERVANT 4: Hi, Job.**
15 **JOB:** *(Downcast)* **Hi, servant.**
16 **SERVANT 4: You look depressed.**
17 **JOB: This has got to be the worst day of my life. First my**
18 **donkeys and oxen got stolen, and then a lightning bolt**
19 **kills all my sheep.**
20 **SERVANT 4: A lightning bolt?**
21 **JOB: Yes. Isn't that strange?**
22 **SERVANT 4: Yeah. Almost as strange as a falling house. He, he,**
23 **he.**
24 **JOB: Exactly! Then someone stole my camels. Can you believe**
25 **that?**
26 **SERVANT 4: Today I can. Uh, listen, Job, I also have news for**
27 **you. But it gets better, and by "better" I mean worse.**
28 **JOB: What happened?**
29 **SERVANT 4: You know how your children all like to get**
30 **together once a month and party all night?**
31 **JOB: Don't tell me they destroyed the furniture again!**
32 **SERVANT 4: Well … the furniture is destroyed, but that's not**
33 **your children's fault.**
34 **JOB: It isn't?**
35 **SERVANT 4: No. The entire house collapsed, and now they're**
36 **all dead.**

1   JOB: All my children are dead?

2   SERVANT 4: But there is some good news to all this.

3   JOB: What's that?

4   SERVANT 4: I'm still alive.

5   JOB: Go away. *(All SERVANTS exit.)* I can't believe it. My
6   beautiful children, all dead! But no matter what, I still
7   love God. *(JOB exits. GOD enters and stands at Center Stage.*
8   *SATAN then enters.)*

9   GOD: Are you here again? Don't you ever quit?

10 SATAN: If you're referring to Job, I saw the whole thing.

11 GOD: I told you he wouldn't let me down. My servant Job has
12   proven to be an honest and blameless man who loves God
13   with his whole heart.

14 SATAN: *(Dismissive wave)* Ha! Anyone will give all he has to
15   save his life, but destroy his health, and he will surely
16   curse you.

17 GOD: OK then, Job is in your power. But you may not kill him.

18 SATAN: Cool. This is going to be fun. *(GOD and SATAN exit.*
19   *JOB enters and stands at Center Stage. SATAN enters with a*
20   *bucket of water or confetti and showers JOB, who screams and*
21   *falls to the ground.)*

22 JOB: Painful sores all over my body. I have never been in such
23   agony! Lord, help me! But no matter what, I still love God.
24   *(GOD runs across stage in victory. SATAN enters, pounds his*
25   *fists on the ground, then exits. JOB's three friends, ELIPHAZ,*
26   *BILDAD, and ZOPHAR enter.)*

27 ELIPHAZ: Job, you look terrible!

28 JOB: It was a sad day when I was born. I've lost everything!

29 ELIPHAZ: Everything? You still have your wife.

30 JOB: Hey, are you here to comfort me or what?

31 ELIPHAZ: Oh yeah, right. Look, Job. You must have done
32   something wrong.

33 BILDAD: Yes, God doesn't punish for no reason.

34 JOB: I've done nothing wrong.

35 ZOPHAR: You know, Job, the sooner you quit lying to yourself,
36   the better. All God wants is a simple apology.

1   JOB: I'm innocent, I tell you. *(Looks up.)* God, why is this
2   happening to me? At least you owe me an explanation.
3   GOD: Enough! *(JOB, ELIPHAZ, BILDAD, and ZOPHAR look*
4   *surprised.)* Job, where were you when I made the earth's
5   foundations? I owe you nothing. No reasons, no
6   explanations. *Nothing!* Even if I gave them, you couldn't
7   understand them. But you are faithful to me, Job. Even
8   though I owe you nothing, I chose to give you everything:
9   renewed health, extra business, and more children, for no
10   one is as righteous as you.
11 JOB: Thank you, God. I will always love you, even if I can't
12   understand why I must go through the things I do. *(ALL*
13   *exit.)*

Where Am I Running?

Theme
Faith, running

Scripture Reference
Hebrews 12:1; 2 Timothy 4:7-8

Synopsis
Two joggers run to finish the course.

Cast
Otter
Zoe

Costumes
Jogging attire

Props
None

Setting
A gym

1   (OTTER *and* ZOE *enter. They face the audience and start to jog*
2   *in place.*)
3   OTTER: How's it going?
4   ZOE: I don't know. I'm not sure I can make this.
5   OTTER: Sure you can. We both agreed that no matter what,
6   we're going to stay the course, remember?
7   ZOE: Finish the race.
8   OTTER: And keep the faith.
9   ZOE: It's just that I need to feel I'm going somewhere.
10   OTTER: The road we travel is a lot longer than you think. You
11   can't expect to know where you're going all the time.
12   ZOE: I guess you're right.
13   OTTER: Of course I'm right. I mean, right now I'm facing a
14   huge hill, but I know I just have to gut it out and continue
15   on the course.
16   ZOE: What hill?
17   OTTER: It's all figurative.
18   ZOE: Oh. Right.
19   OTTER: It's all part of this "faith" issue.
20   ZOE: Running requires faith?
21   OTTER: You know, trusting God to lead you down the right
22   path, knowing that no matter what happens along life's
23   highway, the Lord is in control of our direction.
24   ZOE: Direction is important.
25   OTTER: Absolutely. Don't you feel secure knowing that, like
26   the Apostle Paul said, we are never alone?
27   ZOE: Yes, but —
28   OTTER: We can go up, we can go down, we can turn dangerous
29   corners, run during the heat of day, in the cold or the dark
30   — we can do it all.
31   ZOE: Yes, but —
32   OTTER: I mean, it's a great comfort to know the Lord is always
33   going to be there no matter what road we run.
34   ZOE: I agree, but can we at least get off the treadmill?

Where Do You Fit?

Theme

Spiritual gifts, offering yourself in service to Christ

Scripture Reference

1 Corinthians 12:8-13; Isaiah 11:2-3

Synopsis

How do you know what line of volunteer work
will be the best fit for you?

Cast

Lucy
Arnold
Steward
Angela
Extra

Props

A large hand mirror, table with papers set at Center Stage,
with a sign that says, "Sign up for Volunteer Sunday."

Setting

A church on Volunteer Sunday

Note: The ideas in this sketch are a hodgepodge from my own
personal fascination with the gifts of the Holy Spirit via
the Scripture references, plus Dr. Tim LaHaye's book,
Why You Act the Way You Do, and Bill Gothard's
interpretation of spiritual gifts through the Institute of
Basic Life Principles.

1   (*The STEWARD is behind the table, engaged in a conversation*
2   *with an EXTRA. LUCY and ARNOLD approach the table.*)
3   LUCY: Arnold, there it is! There's the sign-up sheet to teach
4   Sunday school.
5   ARNOLD: I don't know, Lucy. I don't think I'm cut out to teach.
6   I'd like something less stressful. (*Picks up a sheet off the*
7   *table.*) Oh, hey! I can man one of the puppets in the puppet
8   ministry.
9   LUCY: You'll do no such thing. I'll not have you hiding behind
10 some curtain making squeaky voices.
11 ARNOLD: Mabel likes my squeaky voice.
12 LUCY: Mabel is a dog! She likes all sorts of things humans
13 don't like. By the way, have you cleaned up all her
14 "business" in the backyard?
15 ARNOLD: I haven't gotten around to that yet.
16 LUCY: You haven't gotten around to it in three weeks! It's
17 becoming an embarrassment.
18 ARNOLD: What are you going to sign up for?
19 LUCY: I'm not sure. Something that will utilize my superior
20 organizational skills.
21 STEWARD: Good morning. Are you folks going to sign up to
22 volunteer?
23 LUCY: We sure are, only I'm not sure what I should do.
24 STEWARD: Well, let's see where you fit. (*He pulls out a large hand*
25 *mirror, runs it up and down the length of her body, and then looks*
26 *in the mirror.*) I see. Judging by your personality trait, you
27 are a Choleric.
28 LUCY: A Choleric?
29 STEWARD: It's just another way of saying you're a go-getter.
30 LUCY: Yes, that's me!
31 STEWARD: And you seem to have the spiritual gift of
32 knowledge.
33 LUCY: Oh yes, I read the Scriptures every day. I know every
34 Bible story.
35 STEWARD: And you have the spiritual talent of organization
36 as well.

1   LUCY: *(Elbows ARNOLD.)* **What did I tell you? I'm definitely**
2   **administrative quality.**
3   STEWARD: **So by adding all of these together, this says your**
4   **best fit is ... Sunday school teacher.**
5   LUCY: **Say what? You must be mistaken. I don't have the**
6   **personality or the skills for that!**
7   STEWARD: **According to this, you do.**
8   LUCY: **What is that ... thing?**
9   STEWARD: **It's a personality matcher. It tells us what gifts God**
10   **gave you, and where you would fit best in the body of**
11   **Christ.**
12   LUCY: **But — but a Sunday school teacher? I expected**
13   **something much more important.** *(ANGELA enters. She*
14   *stops and listens to the conversation.)*
15   STEWARD: **What's more important than teaching a child about**
16   **Jesus? In Proverbs, King Solomon wrote, "Teach a child**
17   **the way he should go, and when he is old, he will not**
18   **depart from it"** *(Proverbs 22:6).*
19   LUCY: **I'd forgotten about that.**
20   STEWARD: **And even Jesus said, "Let the children come to me,**
21   **for such is the Kingdom of heaven"** *(Mark 10:14).*
22   LUCY: **You're right. Sign me up for Sunday school teacher.**
23   ANGELA: **What about me?**
24   STEWARD: *(Runs the mirror up and down ANGELA.)* **I see you**
25   **have the spiritual gift of faith, and you have a special gift**
26   **of mercy. I can see you're a very loving and compassionate**
27   **person.**
28   ANGELA: **Why, thank you. I do try.**
29   STEWARD: **And it says here that your temperament is**
30   **sanguine. That means you always see the bright side of**
31   **things.**
32   ANGELA: **I do consider a glass half full instead of half empty.**
33   STEWARD: **Therefore, you'd work out best as ...**
34   ANGELA: **A greeter?**
35   LUCY: **A counselor?**
36   STEWARD: **A choir member.**

1   LUCY: How does everything you said make her a singer?
2   STEWARD: It doesn't. But it appears the Lord also gave you a
3   special talent for singing. Go ahead, try a few bars.
4   ANGELA: *(Sings.)* Hark! the herald angels sing ... *(She stops and*
5   *looks surprised.)*
6   STEWARD: You see? That is where you fit best. You're using
7   the natural talent God gave you.
8   LUCY: *(Pulls ARNOLD toward the table.)* What about him? I've
9   got to warn you, he doesn't have much talent.
10 ARNOLD: This is true.
11 STEWARD: *(Runs the mirror up and down ARNOLD.)* Let's see.
12   You have the spiritual gift of wisdom.
13 LUCY: What? He doesn't know half the Scriptures that I know.
14 STEWARD: That's because wisdom isn't related to knowledge.
15   Wisdom is being able to make common-sense decisions.
16 ARNOLD: You know, I remember asking the Lord for wisdom
17   when I was a kid.
18 STEWARD: Excellent. In James 1:5 he says, "If any one of you
19   lacks wisdom, ask God and he will give it to you"
20   *(Author's paraphrase).* It says here you have the spiritual
21   temperament of a Phlegmatic.
22 ARNOLD: What does that mean?
23 STEWARD: It means you're easygoing and you get along well
24   with others, but you're not necessarily motivated to get
25   things started.
26 LUCY: I could have told you that.
27 STEWARD: It looks like you also have the spiritual talent of
28   exhorter! That means you're good at encouraging people.
29   So judging by all this information, I see you fit best as
30   a ...
31 LUCY: Teacher.
32 ANGELA: An usher.
33 STEWARD: An elder *(Or deacon)* and head of our building
34   project.
35 LUCY and ARNOLD: *(Together)* What?!
36 ARNOLD: I can't be in charge of anything.

1   LUCY: I can vouch for that. I'm the one who has to do
2   *everything* around the house, and you're telling me that
3   *he's* the administrator type? Ha!
4   STEWARD: *(To ARNOLD)* With the spiritual temperament of a
5   Phlegmatic, you may not seek responsibility, but once it's
6   thrust upon you, you tend to do a good job. As one with
7   wisdom and the ability to encourage others, you're a
8   natural leader at delegating tasks that fit the personalities
9   of those under you.
10   LUCY: I think something's wrong with that mirror of yours.
11   STEWARD: There are many ways to find your fit, but
12   sometimes the best way is the simplest of all.
13   ANGELA: And what is that?
14   ARNOLD: Oh, I know. Just volunteer your services. The
15   church needs you.
16   STEWARD: *(To Audience)* And that's a wise man speaking.

Who Died and Made You Boss?

Theme
Authority

Scripture Reference
Mark 11:27-33

Synopsis
The Pharisees and Sadducees are feeling a bit threatened
and question Jesus' authority.

Cast
Pharisee
Sadducee
Aide
Extra (man or woman)

Costumes
Biblical robes for all

Props
None

Setting
Jerusalem

1   *(PHARISEE and SADDUCEE stand at Center Stage, talking.)*
2   **PHARISEE:** *(Pointing out over the congregation)* **Look at that Jesus**
3   **person, will you? It's disgraceful how many people glom**
4   **on to him.**
5   **SADDUCEE: Absolutely disgraceful. Where's my aide?** *(AIDE*
6   *enters.)*
7   **AIDE: Wow, you ought to hear what Jesus is preaching about.**
8   **Talk about deep stuff! He speaks like he's an authority on**
9   **the issue. I've never heard anything like it. Why don't you**
10   **two speak like Jesus?**
11   **PHARISEE: Blasphemy. As one of the members of the high**
12   **priesthood and a Pharisee, I make it my personal business**
13   **to remain humble at all times.**
14   **SADDUCEE: Give it a rest. Everyone knows your humility**
15   **went right out the window the moment you put on the**
16   **robe.**
17   **PHARISEE: It's just like a Sadducee to think himself superior**
18   **to others.**
19   **SADDUCEE: And it's just like a Pharisee to think he alone has**
20   **exclusive knowledge of the Word of God.**
21   **AIDE: Since you don't need me anymore, I'm going to listen to**
22   **Jesus.**
23   **SADDUCEE: Hold on, now.** *(Grabs AIDE's robe and pulls him*
24   *back.)* **Ask Jesus this question: "On whose authority do**
25   **you preach and heal?"**
26   **PHARISEE: Oh, good one.**
27   **AIDE: Do I have to? Why can't you guys ask him yourself? I**
28   **kind of like this Jesus person, and I'd hate to get on the**
29   **wrong side of him, just in case I need a miracle someday.**
30   **SADDUCEE:** *(Pushes him.)* **Quit babbling and go!** *(AIDE exits.)*
31   **PHARISEE: You know what I can't stand about Jesus? He had**
32   **the audacity to imply that we actually enjoy walking**
33   **around in our fancy robes and having people greet us and**
34   **talk to us with respect.**
35   **SADDUCEE: Why shouldn't they? After all, we deserve it.**
36   **PHARISEE: It's not vanity. We have a very humbling position.**

1   SADDUCEE: That's right. By the way, you have a hole in the
2   seam of your armpit.
3   PHARISEE: *(Checks his armpit.)* Do I? Drat! Now I'm going to
4   have to get another robe. Good thing Dad has lots of
5   money. *(AIDE enters.)*
6   SADDUCEE: Well, what did he say?
7   AIDE: He wants you to answer a question first. He said, "When
8   John baptized people, was that authority from God, or
9   just from other people?"
10   PHARISEE: Tell him it was from other people.
11   SADDUCEE: No! If we say that, the crowd will turn on us. You
12   know they believe he's a prophet.
13   PHARISEE: OK, fine. Tell him John's authority came from God.
14   SADDUCEE: No, you idiot! If we say that, Jesus will say, "Why
15   didn't you believe him?"
16   PHARISEE: Fine! Then we'll tell him the people gave him
17   authority.
18   SADDUCEE: No! Are you trying to start a riot?
19   PHARISEE: What are we going to do, then? Whichever answer
20   we give him will make us look like idiots.
21   AIDE: *(Giggles.)* It sure does. *(Both the PHARISEE and*
22   *SADDUCEE glare at the AIDE, who lets out a nervous cough.)*
23   SADDUCEE: I want you to tell him that *(Pause)* we don't know.
24   AIDE: OK, but I think you two are wimping out on this one.
25   *(Exits.)*
26   PHARISEE: You know, you really need to get rid of your aide.
27   SADDUCEE: I'd love to, but I can't. He's my wife's relative.
28   PHARISEE: *(Nods understandingly.)* I have one of those as well.
29   *(AIDE enters.)*
30   AIDE: He said that since you don't know, then he won't tell you
31   what authority he has to do these things.
32   PHARISEE: A typical evasive answer.
33   SADDUCEE: You know, this guy's dangerous. The more people
34   follow him, the less power it gives to us.
35   PHARISEE: Before you know it, people won't be giving us the
36   respect we deserve.

1   **SADDUCEE: Oh, I don't think it would ever come to that.**

2   *(EXTRA enters, walking across stage.)* **Good afternoon,**

3   **ma'am.** *(Or sir.)*

4   **EXTRA: Drop dead.** *(Exits.)*

5   **SADDUCEE: At least my faithful aide will listen to me. Isn't**

6   **that right, aide?** *(No answer.)* **Aide?** *(No answer, so he speaks*

7   *even louder.)* **Aide!**

8   **AIDE: I'm sorry — did you say something?**

9   **SADDUCEE: You're right. We need to get rid of him.**

10   **PHARISEE: The sooner the better.** *(Both start to exit.)* **Do these**

11   **robes make me look fat?** *(AIDE watches them go, then exits*

12   *in the other direction toward Jesus.)*

The Whole Two Miles

Theme
Going the extra mile, the Sermon on the Mount

Scripture Reference
Matthew 5:41

Synopsis
A Jewish boy learns a lesson from the Sermon on the Mount.

Cast
Reuben
Naomi
Micah
Soldier

Costumes
A Roman soldier costume and biblical robes for the family

Props
A large bag or backpack, clothes

Setting
The biblical home of Reuben and Naomi

1   *(REUBEN enters stage, obviously looking for someone. NAOMI*
2   *is folding clothes.)*
3   REUBEN: Naomi, have you seen Micah?
4   NAOMI: I sent him to the marketplace this morning
5   REUBEN: That boy was supposed to help me in the shop today,
6   but he never showed up.
7   NAOMI: That's not like him. Do you suppose something
8   happened?
9   REUBEN: If it didn't, he'll be in a whole lot of trouble with me.
10 NAOMI: Now Reuben, he's just a boy.
11 REUBEN: He's twelve-years-old. I expect him to act like a man.
12 NAOMI: This is so unlike him. *(MICAH enters.)*
13 MICAH: Mother, Father, I'm home.
14 REUBEN: Where have you been?
15 MICAH: The Roman soldiers came through town today.
16 NAOMI: Roman soldiers!
17 REUBEN: That hardly explains your tardiness.
18 MICAH: I was standing among the crowd when one of the
19   soldiers pointed at me and demanded I carry his pack.
20 NAOMI: Oh, those miserable men. Why can't they leave us
21   alone?
22 REUBEN: So you carried the pack one mile for him, as required
23   by law?
24 MICAH: No, sir. I carried it two miles.
25 REUBEN: Two miles! They can't do that.
26 NAOMI: That's horrible.
27 MICAH: No, Mother — you don't understand.
28 NAOMI: *(Shakes head.)* Making a boy carry a heavy pack for two
29   miles. You could have permanently injured your back!
30 REUBEN: I'm going to speak to the Head Centurion. They have
31   a strict rule concerning the abuse of this law.
32 NAOMI: I hope he gets beaten.
33 MICAH: Please, Father. He didn't make me go two miles. I
34   volunteered!
35 REUBEN: You *what?* Why would you do such a thing?
36 MICAH: Because of what the Master taught us on the

1   mountain that day.

2   REUBEN: Explain yourself.

3   MICAH: Well, I was standing in the crowd with everyone else,

4   watching the soldiers. I was thinking how much I hate

5   them and their intrusion on our land when the soldier

6   told me I had to carry his pack. It was heavy, too. *(Off to the*

7   *side of stage, a SOLDIER enters.)*

8   SOLDIER: You, boy! Carry my pack. *(MICAH picks up the pack*

9   *and walks along in place with the SOLDIER while still narrating*

10   *the story.)*

11   MICAH: So the first mile I carried his pack, I really hated him

12   for making me do it. But then I remembered what Jesus

13   said on the mountain that day.

14   NAOMI: What did he say?

15   MICAH: "If someone forces you to go a mile, go with him two

16   miles" *(Matthew 5:4)*. That really got me to thinking, and it

17   wasn't long before I made up my mind.

18   SOLDIER: You can put the pack down now.

19   MICAH: That's OK. I'll go another mile.

20   SOLDIER: The law only requires you to carry my pack one

21   mile.

22   MICAH: I know, but I'll carry the pack another mile anyway.

23   REUBEN: I'll bet that surprised him.

24   MICAH: At first we walked in silence. He kept looking at me

25   out of the corner of his eye when he finally asked —

26   SOLDIER: Why are you doing this?

27   MICAH: I explained what Jesus told us that day on the

28   mountain. He was surprised to learn that we're followers

29   of Jesus. He had heard the stories and wondered if they

30   were true. I told him all about how Jesus died on the cross,

31   how he rose from the dead, and how he not only came for

32   the Jews, but for the Romans as well.

33   NAOMI: Did he choose to follow Jesus?

34   MICAH: He didn't say anything out loud, but I could tell I had

35   him thinking. He kept asking questions until we realized

36   we had already gone the extra mile. I gave him the pack,

1   and do you know what he did? He thanked me! *(MICAH*

2   *places the pack down. The SOLDIER shakes his hand. MICAH*

3   *then walks back over to his parents. SOLDIER exits.)*

4   REUBEN: I don't think I've ever heard of a Roman thanking a

5   Jew for anything.

6   MICAH: It was more than just a routine thank you; it was a

7   thank you when someone really appreciates what you

8   said. I looked in his eyes, and I felt a new respect for the

9   man. Who knows? Someday he may even become a

10   brother.

11   REUBEN: Well, you certainly planted the seed, son.

12   NAOMI: And it wouldn't have come to pass if you hadn't

13   listened to the Master that day.

14   MICAH: I didn't realize it until I said it, but Jesus really did die

15   for everyone. He really does love us all. *(ALL exit.)*

The Wisdom of Judy

Theme
Prayer

Scripture Reference
Matthew 5:45

Synopsis
Judy's back with more advice. A businessman has lost the respect of his employees, but Judy's solution is not one he anticipated.

Cast
Judy
Man (Or woman)

Costumes
Professional attire for Judy and a suit for the businessman/woman

Props
A nail file

Setting
Judy's office

1 *(JUDY is standing at Stage Right, filing her nails and looking*
2 *bored. She is used to people asking her questions and responds in*
3 *a deadpan monotone. MAN enters.)*
4 MAN: Judy, I have a problem!
5 JUDY: Have you tried Valium?
6 MAN: What? *(Regains his composure.)* No, nothing like that. I'm
7 CEO of a large corporation, but I'm having difficulty
8 earning the trust of the people beneath me.
9 JUDY: Have you tried yelling at them?
10 MAN: Of course.
11 JUDY: Blaming them for your mistakes?
12 MAN: Every chance I get. I even doubled the workload and
13 decreased the pay. They laughed in my face — what's
14 with that?!
15 JUDY: *(Dismissive wave)* They're just the staff, sir. Have you
16 tried praying with them?
17 MAN: *(Taken aback)* I can't do that. I have a reputation to
18 uphold.
19 JUDY: Prayer does more than you think. It opens barriers,
20 increases communication, and allows Christ to work in
21 the hearts and minds of everyone involved.
22 MAN: Ah, yes — but how do I answer the tough questions? As
23 CEO, I'm sure they'll want to know why God would
24 allow bad things to happen to good people, like —
25 JUDY: Wars and disasters?
26 MAN: Oh, far worse than that.
27 JUDY: Sickness and death?
28 MAN: Worse. How do I explain it when the other company gets
29 that million-dollar contract and not me — *(Quickly)* I
30 mean, us?
31 JUDY: In Matthew 5:45, Jesus says that God sends the sun to
32 shine on the good and the bad, and sends rain on the just
33 and the unjust.
34 MAN: You want me to quote a weather forecast?
35 JUDY: It's just a figure of speech, sir.
36 MAN: But a loving God would never allow bad things to

1   happen or send people to hell.

2   JUDY: A loving God did not send bad things. A loving God

3   sent his son to die for you and pay the ultimate price of

4   sin.

5   MAN: So if I end up in hell —

6   JUDY: You paddle your own canoe.

7   MAN: I beg your pardon?

8   JUDY: You're on your own, because everything has already

9   been done to prevent you from going.

10   MAN: But what if our company doesn't prosper? What if I

11   don't get what I want?

12   JUDY: Then prayer opens the door for asking that God's will be

13   done in your life and the lives of all your employees.

14   MAN: So if we pray together, we'll be able to determine God's

15   direction!

16   JUDY: Exactly, sir.

17   MAN: OK then, I think I'll go pray with them right now, and

18   I'm even going to give them all a raise. *(Stops and places his*

19   *hand to his head.)* Whoa — did I say that out loud? *(Exits.)*

Worrywart

Theme
Worry

Scripture Reference
Matthew 6:25-34

Synopsis
Need worries? Call on the Wart.

Cast
Realtor
Tristan
Smart Alec
Worrywart
Extras (Two)

Costumes
Extras should be dressed in black. Realtor wears a suit. Smart Alec and Worrywart wear signs with their names on them.

Setting
A house that is for sale.

1   *(Scene begins with TRISTAN standing Center Stage, with*
2   *SMART ALEC and WORRYWART on either side.)*
3   REALTOR: *(Enters.)* Hello there.
4   TRISTAN: Hello.
5   REALTOR: I see you're looking at one of our homes for sale.
6   TRISTAN: Yes, I'm interested in buying a place of my own.
7   REALTOR: As you can see, this particular home is in top
8   condition. A former carpenter owned it.
9   TRISTAN: Really? Alec, what do you think?
10   SMART ALEC: It certainly looks sturdy. A carpenter would've
11   taken care of it.
12   TRISTAN: Wart?
13   WORRYWART: I don't know. You know the saying, "Everyone
14   in town has shoes except the shoemaker's kids." How do
15   you know he didn't abuse the place?
16   TRISTAN: *(To REALTOR)* I'm not sure about this place ...
17   WORRYWART: Why did he move all of a sudden?
18   TRISTAN: Why did he up and leave so suddenly?
19   REALTOR: That I can't tell you.
20   WORRYWART: More like he won't tell you.
21   TRISTAN: Do you have anything else?
22   REALTOR: Certainly. Anything you have in mind?
23   TRISTAN: Maybe near the ocean?
24   WORRYWART: *(Sing-song)* Hurricanes!
25   TRISTAN: On top of a hill?
26   WORRYWART: *(Sing-song)* Mud slides!
27   TRISTAN: Away from the water?
28   REALTOR: So you want a home that's close to the water, but
29   away from it?
30   TRISTAN: Yes.
31   REALTOR: Come this way. *(REALTOR leads them across the stage.*
32   *WORRYWART wanders off toward the exit.)* Over here we
33   have a home that overlooks the ocean, but it's on a solid
34   plateau and higher than any surf.
35   SMART ALEC: It looks safe, and it has a great view.
36   TRISTAN: Yes, it may do, but ... *(Looks around)* Wart!

1   (*WORRYWART comes running in.*)

2   REALTOR: Who's Wart?

3   WORRYWART: I was just checking out the roads. Winding,

4   curving roads up to the house means slippery and

5   dangerous during a rain storm.

6   TRISTAN: The view is awesome.

7   WORRYWART: But how are you going to make the payment?

8   What if you lose your job? Oh, I know — we may starve

9   to death, but at least the view's great.

10   SMART ALEC: Oh, come off it. He's got a stable job. Have a

11   little faith!

12   WORRYWART: Two words: foreclosure.

13   SMART ALEC: That's only one word, Wart.

14   WORRYWART: In *your* dictionary, perhaps.

15   TRISTAN: (*To REALTOR*) Do you have anything else?

16   REALTOR: Would you like to live in the city?

17   SMART ALEC: It's close to work.

18   WORRYWART: But the smog will kill you. Can you say lung

19   cancer, anyone?

20   TRISTAN: No city.

21   REALTOR: The country?

22   SMART ALEC: It would be peaceful.

23   WORRYWART: Yeah, but the wild animals carry bubonic

24   plague.

25   TRISTAN: Uh ... no country.

26   REALTOR: An apartment, then?

27   SMART ALEC: Easy care. You won't have to do yard work.

28   WORRYWART: But you won't have any privacy, either.

29   Besides, how do we know it's not gang territory?

30   TRISTAN: I'm sure I could afford a gated community.

31   WORRYWART: Great. So if you're mugged, you can't get out.

32   TRISTAN: I guess no apartment either.

33   REALTOR: Who are you talking to?

34   TRISTAN: (*Introduces them.*) This is Smart Alec, and this is

35   Worrywart.

36   SMART ALEC: Pleased to meet you.

1 WORRYWART: He can't hear you, dummy.

2 TRISTAN: They keep me balanced.

3 REALTOR: Looks like they keep you conflicted. If I were you,

4   I'd keep the smart guy and ditch the worrywart.

5 WORRYWART: Don't listen to that sadist. He's only interested

6   in a sale.

7 SMART ALEC: He's got sound advice. You *are* a nuisance at

8   times.

9 WORRYWART: See? He's poisoning your mind already.

10 TRISTAN: But if I get rid of my worries, I won't have anything

11   to ... worry about.

12 SMART ALEC: That's the idea.

13 REALTOR: You know, I used to have a worrywart too.

14 TRISTAN: Really?

15 REALTOR: Oh, sure. But the more I fed him, the stronger he

16   became. Pretty soon I worried about everything in my life.

17   He really paralyzed me.

18 TRISTAN: What did you do?

19 REALTOR: I read the verse in the Bible about how I shouldn't

20   worry about things. I learned that God is big enough to

21   take care of all my needs.

22 WORRYWART: Don't listen to him. He has no idea how

23   stressful your life is.

24 SMART ALEC: But if we rely on God for our daily needs, we

25   won't have to expend the emotional energy to keep the

26   Worrywart around.

27 TRISTAN: You're right. I'm going to give my worries to God

28   and start trusting him to take care of my life. *(Two EXTRAS*

29   *dressed in black enter. They each grab WORRYWART under the*

30   *arm and drag him Off-stage.)*

31 WORRYWART: No. No! You'll miss me, I tell you. Take me

32   back! I'll make you proud of meee!

33 REALTOR: How do you feel?

34 TRISTAN: Like a new person. *(Pause)* I think. *(Pause)* Yeah, like

35   a new person.

36 REALTOR: So, have you decided where you want to live?

1   TRISTAN: The ocean, I think. *(Pauses.)* **Maybe not.** *(Pauses.)* **No,**
2   I think that's where I want to live.
3   SMART ALEC: Wart, where did you hide your brother?
4   WORRYWART: *(Off-stage)* I'm not telling!
5   SMART ALEC: Come on, Tristan — we've got to find a way to
6   get rid of doubt. *(Starts to push him toward the exit.)*
7   TRISTAN: I don't have doubt. At least I don't think I do, do I?
8   REALTOR: Just give it to God, man. Give it to God.

Scripture Reference Index

Scripture	Sketch	Page
Matthew		
16:26	Interview with a Grump	84
23:25-28	Pharisee Cleanser	116
23:27	Hypocritically Speaking	72
28:19-20	How Healthy Are Your Five Parts? — Part 5	69
Mark		
4:3-20	Planting on the Highway	120
11:27-33	Who Died and Made You Boss?	164
16:24	Fix-it Man	30
Luke		
8:11-15	Planting on the Highway	120
21:14-18	How Healthy Are Your Five Parts? — Part 4	65
John		
3:14-16	The Greatest Risk on Earth	52
3:16	Planting on the Highway	120
3:18-21	Double Jeopardy	22
3:19-21	Campaign Promises	16
4:14	I Only Eat Chocolate for the Health Benefits	80
4:35-38	How Healthy Are Your Five Parts? — Part 5	69
8:1-11	Hypocritically Speaking	72
10:10	The Path of Most Resistance	111
12:25	Interview with a Grump	84
14:2	Art in Heaven	6
15:12-13	The Greatest Risk on Earth	52
Acts		
2:4	Quest for Fire	128

Theme Index

About the Author

M. K. Boyle, like J. K. Rowling, e. e. Cummings, G. K. Chesterton, and other double-initialed authors, writes in a specific style with a target audience in mind — in her case, humorous drama for church congregations. She has been acting up in church all her life, with twenty-five of those years devoted to writing and enacting sketches. Traveling with a Christian drama company gave her invaluable experience as a writer and performer.

She is a member of the Christian Writers' Guild. Her published work includes several sketch collections for Advent and a book, *Acting Up in Church*. This is her second book.

Order Form

Meriwether Publishing Ltd.
PO Box 7710
Colorado Springs, CO 80933-7710
Phone: 800-937-5297   Fax: 719-594-9916
Website: www.meriwether.com

Please send me the following books:

_____ **Acting Up in Church AGAIN #BK-B322** $15.95
by M.K. Boyle
More humorous sketches for worship services

_____ **Acting Up in Church #BK-B282** $15.95
by M.K. Boyle
Humorous sketches for worship services

_____ **Worship Sketches 2 Perform #BK-B242** $15.95
by Steven James
A collection of scripts for two actors

_____ **More Worship Sketches 2 Perform** $14.95
#BK-B258
by Steven James
A collection of scripts for two actors

_____ **Service with a Smile #BK-B225** $15.95
by Daniel Wray
52 humorous sketches for Sunday Worship

_____ **The Human Video Handbook #BK-B289** $15.95
by Kimberlee R. Mendoza
Christian outreach in dramatic movement and music

_____ **Christmas on Stage #BK-B153** $19.95
edited by Theodore O. Zapel
An anthology of Christmas plays for all ages

**These and other fine Meriwether Publishing books are available at
your local bookstore or direct from the publisher. Prices subject to
change without notice. Check our website or call for current prices.**

Name: _____ email:_____

Organization name: _____

Address: _____

City: _____ State: _____

Zip: _____ Phone: _____

❏ **Check enclosed**

❏ **Visa / MasterCard / Discover / Am. Express #** _____

Signature: _____   *Expiration
date:*   _____ / _____
(required for credit card orders)

Colorado residents: Please add 3% sales tax.
Shipping: Include $3.95 for the first book and 75¢ for each additional book ordered.

❏ *Please send me a copy of your complete catalog of books and plays.*

Order Form

Meriwether Publishing Ltd.
PO Box 7710
Colorado Springs, CO 80933-7710
Phone: 800-937-5297 Fax: 719-594-9916
Website: www.meriwether.com

Please send me the following books:

_____ **Acting Up in Church AGAIN #BK-B322** $15.95
by M.K. Boyle
More humorous sketches for worship services

_____ **Acting Up in Church #BK-B282** $15.95
by M.K. Boyle
Humorous sketches for worship services

_____ **Worship Sketches 2 Perform #BK-B242** $15.95
by Steven James
A collection of scripts for two actors

_____ **More Worship Sketches 2 Perform** $14.95
#BK-B258
by Steven James
A collection of scripts for two actors

_____ **Service with a Smile #BK-B225** $15.95
by Daniel Wray
52 humorous sketches for Sunday Worship

_____ **The Human Video Handbook #BK-B289** $15.95
by Kimberlee R. Mendoza
Christian outreach in dramatic movement and music

_____ **Christmas on Stage #BK-B153** $19.95
edited by Theodore O. Zapel
An anthology of Christmas plays for all ages

**These and other fine Meriwether Publishing books are available at
your local bookstore or direct from the publisher. Prices subject to
change without notice. Check our website or call for current prices.**

Name: _____ email:_____

Organization name: _____

Address: _____

City: _____ State: _____

Zip: _____ Phone: _____

❑ **Check enclosed**

❑ **Visa / MasterCard / Discover / Am. Express #** _____

Expiration
Signature: _____ *date:* _____ / _____
      (required for credit card orders)

Colorado residents: Please add 3% sales tax.
Shipping: Include $3.95 for the first book and 75¢ for each additional book ordered.

❑ *Please send me a copy of your complete catalog of books and plays.*